The End of the Food Chain

A play

Tim Firth

Samuel French — London
New York - Toronto - Hollywood

THE END OF THE FOOD CHAIN

First performed at the Stephen Joseph Theatre in the Round, Scarborough, in December 1993 with the following cast:

Bruce	Stephen Tompkinson
Ewan	Mark Benton
Dids	David MacCreedy
Robbo	Alan Stocks
Craig	Paul McCrink
Debbie	Michelle Butterly

Directed by Connal Orton
Designed by Jan Bee Brown
Lighting by Jackie Staines
Music by John Pattison

The action of the play takes place in the Kale Moor Grocery Distribution Depot

Time — the present

AUTHOR'S NOTES

The Set

Kale Moor is a grocery distribution depot. From the outside it's just another vast warehouse on the Sponden Industrial Estate. On the inside it's rather like walking into a supermarket and immediately shrinking to one sixth your normal size. Because Kale Moor is the place where supermarkets go to shop. The aisles stretch off into the distance six times further than you're used to. The shelves are six times higher. And as you walk down, the food on the shelves is packaged up in bulk sixty times more than you need.

During the day the sheer size of this place is impressive enough. At night, when there are not many people around, it starts to have the rather bright, empty chill of Jack Nicholson's remote hotel in *The Shining*. And who works here at night? Well, the pickers. Armed with their flotillas of picking cages (hand-pushed trolleys) and lists of little sticky labels they go shopping for all the Delderfield's supermarkets in the leafy middle-class suburbs of neighbouring towns. Delderfield's, by the way, are the kind you find when local residents object to anything so base as a Kwik Save. The shelf-stackers there wear waistcoats and have metal name-badges, rather than a square of plastic with "My name is Mark" scribbled on with a freezer pen.

And who are the pickers at Kale Moor? Well, put it this way. You know how there was always one kid in your class who either pratted about permanently or sat round vacantly like something off a prehistoric sea-bed, and you always thought "I wonder what happens to him"?

The warehouse is divided vertically into "bins" — the bottom bits where the pickers pick — and "reserves" — the bits above where the bulk is stacked before it replenishes the bins. Dexion is everywhere, caging everything, stretching up into the heavens. And everywhere we are distracted by the mouthwatering attractions of excess, intensely concentrated pockets of recognizable yummy foods sitting on pallets stretching down long corridors. In fact there's a sense of "food, food everywhere, but not a drop to eat".

The various scenes move between three levels: the Depot (floor level); the Catwalk and Fifth Reserve (the top of the warehouse, sixty feet up), and the Roof, with its skylights, fans and views over night-time Stockport. The design challenge of this play is to move the action up and down between these levels; not only that, but the transitions between these three areas have to be made with as close to the immediacy of a film "cut" as is possible. Tricky.

It beomes a joint challenge for set and lighting design. In the Scarborough production Jan Bee Brown was faced with a theatre in the round where protecting sightlines precluded building permanent high scaffolding in the centre of the stage, so she fringed the main playing area with pallets, put bulk food (which could be "picked" as part of the action) on them, then put pallets on top of the food at a height of about four feet, so the actors could sit, climb and jump on them. Jackie Staines then underlit these when we cut from Depot to Catwalk to create the illusion of height; the actors had only to step on to the pallets, the lighting state changed and we were sixty feet up. And the roof ... well, mercifully this is a nocturnal play, so skylights could be trucked on to illuminate the night with light from down in the depot.

You will notice occasional references to the "pesto sauce". This is the only higher level physically present on stage; eight feet or so tall, it could be climbed on as part of the action and then ingeniously trucked out from the side to form the "Fifth Reserve" at the climax of the play. Generally, however, relying on lighting rather than logistics enabled Connal Orton, the director, to keep the scene changes as fast as possible.

The "picking cages" were simply those high-sided trolleys commonly used by shelf-stackers in supermarkets, and Debbie's truck was a cunningly converted little battery-powered buggy.

Interrupted Speeches

A speech usually follows the one before it BUT:

When one character starts speaking before the other has finished, the point of interruption is marked /.

e.g. **Craig** The poem doesn't / matter. I was showing the technique ...
      Ewan Is there a poem for javelin?

Ages

The characters are all in their early to mid-twenties.

SYNOPSIS OF SCENES

ACT I
SCENE 1   The Depot. Tuesday night
SCENE 2   The Depot
SCENE 3   The Depot
SCENE 4   The Depot
SCENE 5   The Depot
SCENE 6   The Depot. Wednesday night
SCENE 7   The Catwalk
SCENE 8   The Depot
SCENE 9   The Catwalk
SCENE 10   The Depot
SCENE 11   The Roof
SCENE 12   The Depot. Thursday night

ACT II
SCENE 1   The Depot. Thursday night
SCENE 2   The Depot
SCENE 3   The Catwalk
SCENE 4   The Depot
SCENE 5   The Roof
SCENE 6   The Depot
SCENE 7   The Fifth Reserve and Catwalk
SCENE 8   The Depot. Friday night

Dedicated to
Sarah McDonald
and
Keith Miller
for their inspiration

and to
my Dad
for that terrible night on
Piccadilly railway station

ACT I

SCENE 1

The Depot. Tuesday night

The Lights come up on our central area revealing a clump of pickers, "clump" being the collective noun: Bruce, Ewan, Dids, Robbo and Craig in his sad sports vest. All are attired in safety boots but otherwise have scant regard to the regulation blue overalls and have customized them individually. They are silent, as though recently bereaved. Then after a measured pause, Bruce looks up

Bruce So. Did anyone see him actually get hit?
Ewan (*shaking his head sadly*) There was a hail of crossfire. It could've been any one of us.
Dids He must've been caught by a ricochet.

Pause

Bruce Where did it get him?
Craig (*pointing*) Here. Right on the temple.
Bruce (*wincing*) Ff-ff.
Craig I saw the marks when they stretchered him out.
Bruce Poor old Glen.
Ewan Did you tell the ambulancemen what happened?
Bruce No. No. In the end I didn't think it was fair.
Ewan (*nodding*) On Glen.
Bruce No, on the hospital. It's a very difficult call to make. Having to ring someone's wife at four in the morning to say their husband's been hit by a frozen Brussels sprout.
Craig Will they know, though? At the hospital?
Bruce (*turning slowly*) I doubt it, Craig. I don't think they automatically swab for traces of vegetable.
Craig No / but ——
Ewan It's not a very common condition.
Bruce You think how many times in a hospital you've seen signs for the "sprout-related injuries" wing.
Dids (*looking up*) Eh — it doesn't mean we have to stop playing sprout tag.

Bruce Well it / looks ——

Dids I'm telling y'. Sprout tag is the best game you've come up with. It's solid adrenalin. We're not stopping playing it 'cause some wet git fell out the (*he nods upwards*) pesto sauce and broke his leg.

Bruce No ——

Dids Glen got hit. He lost. He couldn't keep up.

Bruce In fairness to Glen, Dids, sprout tag was always envisaged as a game of stealth and precision using a single Brussels sprout. Not as an apocalyptic barrage resembling the end of *Butch Cassidy and the Sundance Kid.* Which is how it ended up. And all I'm / saying ——

Dids It was solid adrenalin.

Bruce It was solid adrenalin, Dids, I'll give you that. All I'm saying is we tread a fine line here, lads. One more industrial injury and the shift managers (*he points God-ward*) are going to start doubting whether we are responsible little pickers and start bobbing down out of the little office in the sky every five minutes. And that will mean no more games.

Ewan For ever.

Bruce Finito. So I think in our long-term interests, we ought to declare this warehouse a sprout-free zone. Mm?

Ewan (*nodding to the troops*) Mm?

Pause

All Mmr.

Craig (*pleadingly*) But still some games, yeh?

Bruce (*turning to Craig, a smile forming*) Craig. Is this not Kale Moor Distribution Depot? Is it not three in the morning? Is my name not Bruce Kenny? (*He smiles and with his characteristic hand-rub gives his characteristic noise*) Wha-hey!

On this, almost jumping us out of our seats, we are plunged into "Eye of the Tiger" as if this was a Las Vegas boxing match

Black-out

Scene 2

The Depot

The music continues

The Lights snap up on Bruce, in high octane game mode. His enthusiasm makes us feel enthusiastic. He is singing "Eye of the Tiger"; the music ends as he speaks

Bruce Are we read-y?
Ewan ⎱ *(together; off)* Yo!
Dids ⎰
Bruce Good eh! Wha-hey! (*He swings up into the pesto sauce with some panache and presses the nearby shift bell*) Ladies and Gentlemen! The main event on your cards for the undisputed championship and the non-existent Kale Moor trophy, between, in the blue cage, weighing one-eighty pounds, Ian "Robbo" Robinson. Yesss.

In comes Robbo from one aisle, blindfolded with a scarf, in a picking cage pushed by Ewan

Robbo Are we there?
Bruce Shush. And in the red cage, weighing one-forty pounds, Craig "tragically no nickname" Cleminson.

In clanks Craig blindfolded similarly, and swung round like a dervish in his cage by Dids

Craig *Don't swing it round, Dids. I hate the waltzers. Seriously.*
Bruce OK, seconds, your contestants on the marks please.

Dids and Ewan get Craig and Robbo out of their cages

Bruce Blindfolds in place?

Dids and Ewan check the blindfolds

Dids ⎱ *(together)* Yep.
Ewan ⎰
Bruce Hands in pockets?
Dids ⎱ *(together)* Yep.
Ewan ⎰

Bruce OK. (*He pauses slightly*) Then can we have the frozen rainbow trout please?

Dids and Ewan produce two small frozen fish and place their tails in the mouths of the contestants so that most of the fish is sticking out

OK, you know the rules. Completely deprived of the sense of sight, you are attempting to deliver a clop on the head to your opponent. The first to deliver three clops is the winner. Are you ready?

Craig
Robbo } (*together*) Mmg.

Bruce Seconds out!

Dids
Ewan } (*together*) Seconds out!

Bruce Three, two, one — play.

Craig and Robbo clumsily attempt, staying on their marks, to land a clop on the other's head with the fish. The two seconds stand in the cages, hands neatly behind their backs

Good start there by Craig on the left, very good, methodical start, he's manœuvring the fish well, Robbo fencing left to right, none of the technique of Craig's angular, jabbing movements, you'd never believe this is the first time he's played this. Really fabulous fluid action from Craig here, he's really making all the headway …

Suddenly, apparently from nowhere, Dids produces a third frozen trout and whops Craig on the head

Craig Argh. (*He pulls the blindfold off*) Bloody hell!

But all he sees is Robbo, blindfolded, with a trout in his mouth

Bruce Oh what a strike. What a strike there from Robbo. Out of the blue, came out of nowhere.

Robbo (*staring round like Stevie Wonder*) Did I get him?

Ewan You got him.

Robbo (*gripping his fists*) Whurrr.

Bruce That was just ... oi! Come on Craig, blindfold on please.

Craig Bloody hell.

Bruce That's got the crowd buzzing here. OK. Three, two, one ... go.

They start again

And straight away Craig's back at him, what a fighter.

Craig (*really straining*) Nrr … grrr … grrr …

Bruce You can see all that athletics training's paid off. You can just see all that time he's spending at this athletics club is really coming into use here. It's lovely to watch the angular, jabbing movements of this young ——

Dids delivers another clop

Craig Argh, bloody hell.

Bruce Oh, out of the blue again. He's like a cobra.

Robbo Did I get him?

Bruce The man is like a cobra.

Ewan Doing great, Robbo.

Robbo (*gripping his fists*) Whurrr.

Craig But how's he doing / it ——

Bruce He's like a cobra, mate. It's frightening to watch, up here. I thought you did speed training.

Craig I do do speed training.

Bruce Well use it. Come on! Speed! Get in there like lightning.

Dids Go!

Craig swings round to be egged on by Dids and Ewan, and charges himself up

Craig Go!

Bruce Come on. Fast.

Craig (*psyched up*) Yeh! Go! Go!

Bruce Ready?

Craig I'm ready! Three, two, one GO!

Within a nano-second he is again clopped by Dids

Ug.

Bruce (*erupting*) *He's a rattlesnake! The man is a rattlesnake! He has stormed this arena here tonight.* The man whose parents died in a plane crash and was brought up by Amazonian tree lizards has finally come good.

Robbo (*still blindfolded, one arm up in triumph, like Rocky*) Whurr!

Bruce And that, ladies and gentlemen, is the picture that'll be in tomorrow's papers.

Black-out

SCENE 3

The Depot

The Lights come up on Bruce and Ewan picking (which involves sticking labels on to various items of food and loading them into the cages). Dids is reading a magazine called "Muscle and Fitness" and Craig is rather tragically holding the three frozen fish

Craig Ohhh. There were three fish. (*He turns and smiles awkwardly*) Ah that's a really good one that is, Bruce.

Bruce You know what the really tragic thing is? That Robbo genuinely thought he'd done it. Without having made any physical contact at all, we tell him he's won and he goes (*mimicking*) "Whurr!" I mean.

Ewan Tragic.

Bruce It is tragic. It makes you wonder if we rushed up to him with a yellow jersey and said "Robbo mate, y've just won the Tour de France" he'd go (*mimicking*) "Have I? Whurr!"

Craig That's a dead clever one. That's like that one where I kept slapping the back of my head for ages, but y'd actually taken the ten p off.

Ewan What it is, I reckon, is that when he went into Halfords to buy his car stereo, he went up to the counter and said ——

Bruce Whurr. I've just won the Tour de France.

Ewan No, 'cause at this stage he was all right, y' see.

Bruce Oh right.

Ewan He said, "Can I try out your extensive range of car stereos?" And they said, "Certainly sir, just put on the relevant stereophonic headphones". But due to a tragic cock-up, the first pair he put on weren't headphones, they were in fact those things they put on cattle to stun them in abattoirs.

Bruce Which meant the true tragedy was that at the same moment, an Aberdeen Angus in an abattoir somewhere was approaching some rotating knives thinking "Why did that bloke just play me a bit of Burt Bacharach?"

Craig (*trying to keep up*) Yeh!

Bruce Or, (*he points*) at a birthday party at the age of six, someone tragically forgot to give the command "*Simon says* you can return to a normal human being" and went straight on to musical chairs. Thus condemning Robbo to a life of bovine misery.

Craig What's bovine?

Bruce points at Ewan, automatically

Bruce "What is bovine?" Ewan.

Ewan (*very quickly and automatically*) What bograpes grow on, Bruce.

Bruce Ten points.

Bruce and Ewan have evolved a gesture to accompany the awarding of points. They do it

Craig Don't go into loads of made up answers again, seriously. What's /
  it ——
Bruce Like a cow, Craig.
Ewan Ovine is like a sheep.
Bruce Vulpine is a like a fox.
Craig I didn't know there were words like that. Is there one for every animal?
Bruce (*heaving a unit*) Well, all the major ones. I think by the time you get down to llamas the necessity drops out.
Craig Right.
Ewan Very rarely do you ever see anything that makes you think "That's a bit like a llama."
Bruce Except another llama.
Ewan In which case you'd probably just say: "There's a llama."
Bruce True.
Ewan (*pointing*) That's probably the only occasion you'd use it.
Craig But I mean Margaret Thatcher's like that now, isn't she?
Bruce What, like a llama?
Craig It was on the telly.
Ewan If she looks like a llama I'm not surprised she was on the telly.
Bruce Ten points.

They do their gesture again

Craig No, I mean she's got a word — three words named after her in this new Oxford English Dictionary. I mean, that, having words — where you become a word. I mean y've just done it then, haven't you?
Bruce What?
Craig In your life, y've done it. Cracked it. If y've become a word, that's it.
Ewan Well y' have to be careful with that, y' see. There's a difference between someone saying something at a dinner party and being called a "Thatcherite", and someone being repeatedly hit on the head with a frozen fish and everyone saying "You sodding great Craig."
Craig (*smiling awkwardly*) Yeh, well I mean in the right way, obviously. I mean, like, Bruce. Wouldn't you like to have "Brucite" in the Oxford English Dictionary?
Bruce No, because it sounds like a type of coal.
Craig "Brucian", then. To be that important / that you ——
Ewan I hope y'r not implying you're not important already, Craig.

Craig Well, no / I ——
Ewan You do realize the gravity of your function here.
Craig No / I ——
Ewan You do realize, one slip with one of these stickers and tomorrow the people of Buxton will have no Crunchie?
Craig No / but ——
Bruce There'll just be a gap on the shelf.
Craig I know / but ——
Ewan You hold Buxton's Crunchie in your grasp.
Craig What I / mean ——
Bruce D' you ever think — why is it always the "Oxford" English Dictionary.
Craig (*left behind on the track now*) Eh?
Bruce Why isn't there a Manchester English Dictionary? I wonder what that'd be like.
Ewan Very slim.
Bruce I'd love to see the entry under "Liverpool".
Ewan "Small city in the North West of England that thinks it's a bloody massive city in the North West of England."
Craig You see?
Ewan Comes from the Latin "Liver", to nick, and "pool", car stereo.
Craig Y' see, that'd be "Brucian".
Bruce (*turning*) Eh?
Craig Like what Ewan was saying then. That'd be "Brucian".

They all look at Craig

Suddenly in comes Robbo with his picking cage

Bruce Wha-hayy! It's the flashing blade!
Ewan Who is that masked swordsman?
Bruce It's not a mask.
Ewan What a tragedy.
Bruce I shall now free Robbo from fifteen years of drudgery. (*He stands, grandly*) Robbo, Simon says return to a normal human being. (*He clicks his fingers*)

Robbo looks at Bruce. There is a pause

Robbo I need two units of Fudge for Glossop.
Bruce What a phenomenal let-down.
Craig Yeh!
Robbo (*reading stickers*) Aisle C, bin twelve, position ... (*he squints*)

Dids and Ewan immediately turn

Dids (*not looking up*) B. Cadbury's Fudge, boxes of forty-eight.

Ewan Aisle A, bin four, position A?

Dids (*not looking up*) Sunquest orange, cases of sixteen.

Bruce Aisle F, bin nine, position A.

Dids (*not looking up*) Kattomeat, turkey, cases of twenty-four.

Ewan You know, people who say body-builders are thick just haven't questioned Dids on the layout of Kale Moor ambient grocery depot.

Dids Very good.

Ewan He seriously ought to think about *Mastermind*, don't y' reckon?

Dids (*not looking up*) Very good.

Ewan The only problem'd be the general knowledge round. He'd have to just sit and wait for a question to come up on press-ups.

Robbo C twelve B.

Dids (*to Ewan, quietly*) Funny man.

Bruce The thing is, Dids, have you ever seen what a body-builder looks like at the age of sixty?

Dids (*sighing*) No.

Bruce No, neither have I. Interesting implications there, don't you think?

Craig Yeh, and what's the recipe page in a body-building magazine? Is it like this plate with four syringes on it?

Dids No, Craig, it isn't. Like I told Bruce two weeks ago when he made that syringes joke, and it was funny. But it's not funny coming out of your gob, 'cause the only thing that'd be funny coming out of your gob is your teeth, very fast.

Craig (*very quietly*) Why don't y' shut yours, Dids.

Dids (*looking up*) Pardon?

Craig Bruce, do / you ——

Dids I said pardon, Craig?

Bruce (*leaping up to intervene*) Dids. Down.

Dids lowers himself

Don't take him on. I know you can bench press two hundred kilos and punch straight through sheet metal, but you have to remember Craig here (*he points*) has a sporty vest.

Craig Athletics vest. It's an athletics vest. That's an athletics badge. Three As star award.

Dids Whose track suit did that fall off?

Craig It's mine. I got awarded this! It's Three As grade one. For discus.

Dids To get Three As grade one, y' just have to be able to put y'r track suit on the right way out.

Craig No / it's not ——

Dids They give you one if y' can tell the difference between a discus and a carrot.

Craig You have to get it over twenty-eight metres.

Ewan Throwing or carrying?

Craig Throwing.

Bruce Yeh, without being rude, Craig, I keep hearing these stories of you at this athletics club and my basic problem is that most discus throwers I've ever seen look like Greek gods whereas you look more like something they stick in the ground to mark where a discus has landed.

Craig Yeh, well, that's because size isn't important. What's important for discus is speed. That's what my instructor gets us training for. Getting y'r whole body coiled up like a tensed spring.

Bruce Really?

Ewan And is he coiled up like a spring?

Craig No / well—

Bruce He must have terrible trouble finding trousers.

Craig I / mean—

Ewan If you push down on his head does he stay there for three seconds then spring ninety feet into the air?

Craig I mean coiled vertically around the central ... (*He points, joyfully*) I'll show you!

Craig rushes off

There is a communal sigh

Dids (*in a disgusted mutter*) Ohh ...

Ewan That's your fault. What did they tell you at the zoo?

Bruce (*closing his eyes and slapping his wrist*) Humour him but don't show any interest.

Robbo I need two units of Fudge for Glossop.

Bruce and Ewan spring up

Bruce My God. You see I'd forgotten him.

Ewan I'd forgotten him.

Bruce That's why the man is so lethal at sprout tag. Natural camouflage. Still for half a minute and he blends in with inert groceries.

Robbo We're not playing sprout tag, are we?

Bruce No, Robbo (*he reaches to a bin*) we're doing some work, mate. We're getting you two units of Fudge so that you can go to bed this morning with a glow of pride knowing you have played a part in the tooth decay of Glossop's schoolchildren. Catch.

Bruce throws one unit of Fudge to Robbo

Robbo Are we playing sprout tag now?
Ewan He is fascinating really. He is the human equivalent of a fax machine. If he doesn't get an answer the first time, he goes on to automatic redial.
Bruce (*throwing a second unit*) Glossop's Fudge, my lord. Handle it carefully.

As the Fudge flies across the stage, Craig thunders back in mid-throw with a boxed flan base

Craig OK. Watch out, Robbo. Right. (*He opens the flan base box*) Just watch out the way, Robbo. Right, are y' ready? Move back.

The others move back, as parents do for a child

Ewan Why is it whenever I watch Craig doing something, I can somehow hear this kazoo playing.
Craig Right now, the circle is about here (*he marks a circle with his foot*) round, OK. And this flan base is the discus, OK. Only in real life it's two kilograms. And what a lot of people don't ... OK, what way d' you think the discus comes out of the thrower's hand?

Pause

Bruce You know you were asking me this same question last night?
Ewan And we prayed that one day some bloke would come along with a flan base and show us?
Craig The front.
Ewan The front!
Craig Most people think it's the back.
Bruce I said the back.
Ewan I said you put it in your mouth and slap y'r cheeks.
Craig So (*he gets into position*) you stand with your hand over it, at the back of the circle, OK. And this is where you get the first poem.
Ewan Poem?
Bruce Well, now I am interested.
Ewan What poem?
Craig (*taking a stance*) Right. (*He coughs. Proudly, as if reciting a bit of Milton*) "Arm head spine. In a line. You're doing fine."

The others look at him

OK? That gets you at right angles. Then you move round to the centre spot (*he does, awkwardly*) and this is where you get the second poem. "Chin knee toe. Make a bow. See it go" — argh. (*He lets go of the flan base, which flops on to the floor*)

There is a slight pause

Ewan Leading to the final poem. "Head foot knee. Arm nose leg. Can you help me I'm tangled up in the discus net."
Craig No, I've never / done ——
Bruce (*smiling*) Ten points.

The gesture

Craig No, I've never done that. If you go out of the circle it's a no-throw ...
Bruce I had no idea poetry played such an important part in athletics.
Craig Eh?
Robbo That wasn't a poem.
Craig The poem doesn't / matter ——
Robbo It only had three lines.
Craig The poem doesn't / matter. I was showing the technique ...
Ewan Is there a poem for javelin?
Bruce "Pick it up, run dead fast. Chuck it."
Craig I was showing / the technique ——
Ewan Ah, blank verse then.
Craig Bruce!
Bruce Not always. Fatima Whitbread used to run up shouting, "I must go down to the sea again, to the lonely sea and sky-yyyyy ... "
Craig Look it was the technique! The poem didn't matter — it's the technique, all right? That I was showing. That's how I got it twenty-eight metres thirty-four. How I got the star. How I got this. (*He points to his badge*)

There is a pause

Bruce Sorry, Craig.
Ewan Sorry, Craig.
Dids (*shaking his head; quietly*) Bloody tragic.

Black-out

SCENE 4

The Depot

The Lights come up. Bruce and Ewan are lying on the concrete floor at opposite ends of the stage. C is the flan case. Somewhere there is a unit of standard Smartie tubes with its contents gaping

Ewan tiddly-winks a Smartie with a tube lid. It skitters sadly across the floor

Ewan The problem is. Once y've tasted the sheer adrenalin-pumped excitement of sprout tag, it's very hard to get excited about landing a Smartie in a flan case.

Bruce Listen, mate. There's people lying in railway arches now with their arms full of drugs saying, "I wish I could still get a high from landing a Smartie in a flan case". (*He pings another Smartie*)

Bruce and Ewan move in for the next shot

Ewan I very much doubt anyone's ever said that.

Bruce Y' see, man has a basic inability to remain satisfied. Today's adrenalin is tomorrow's boredom. It's the reason the adolescent boy who's discovered manual stimulation and thinks it's the best thing in the world, five years later can't get excited unless he paints his fingernails red and pretends it's Jane Seymour.

Ewan Y've never done that, have you?

Bruce What?

Ewan Pretended it was Jane Seymour.

Bruce Naa. Tragically we didn't have any nail varnish at our house. No, I used to put my hand in an oven glove and pretend it was one of the Muppets.

Ewan Now that is a *damn* good idea.

Bruce No, but it's true. Example, OK. School, second year. I discovered one health education lesson that if you took the tube out of a biro, OK, and chewed a bit of paper, then y' could fire it like a blowpipe. (*He mimes this*)

Ewan Really?

Bruce Oh, I cannot express the happiness I got out of this, Ewan. Honestly. After eight months the ceiling of our prefab looked like it'd been artexed, I'd got 'em everywhere. But then I had to go looking for the bigger kick, didn't I, y' see? Had to start putting pins in the paper. Then dipping the pins in ink ——

Ewan Right ...

Bruce Before I know it I'm in before the headmaster explaining why this first year has died of blood poisoning with a half-completed tattoo of Guadeloupe on his back.

Ewan (*pointing*) But it's a talent.

Bruce Oh, I know. When I used to have the annual post-parents' evening rows with my dad I'd get me blowpipe out and say, "What d'you mean I've wasted your money and achieved nothing? You try hitting the second hand on the biology clock with that."

Ewan Did he have a go?

Bruce He never tried.

Ewan Pathetic.

Bruce I offered to let him stand closer and everything. (*He pings a Smartie*) No, he normally took the tack of (*mimicking*) "Why, oh, why can't you have your little sister's attitude?" And who was right?

Ewan Who was right?

Bruce What happened to our Ruth?

Ewan What happened to our Ruth?

Bruce She went to university, got a degree, got a job with the VAT ... is she satisfied, Ewan?

Ewan Is she, Bruce?

They lean in conspiratorially

Bruce (*pointing*) Somewhere out there, across the milky way of lights that is Stockport, there is a little mock-Georgian-fronted house with my little sister Ruth in it, currently (*he checks his watch*) hosting one of her Jill and Clive and Steve and Emma dinner parties. OK, two years ago, just a "dinner party" would have been enough. Tonight, they are having a "murder mystery dinner party" which she bought in a box from Kendal's, where they all have to pretend they're a different character all evening, deliver clues and guess who's the murderer. Now that is the suburban equivalent of narcotic abuse.

Ewan It is.

Bruce Because what happens when that's not enough?

Ewan Where's she going to end up?

Bruce Under the railway arch next to the bloke saying, "I wish I could still get ——"

Ewan ⎱ (*together*) "—— a high from landing a Smartie in a flan case."
Bruce ⎰

Ewan Tragic.

Bruce It is tragic. No, the ability to focus down your sources of excitement in life is a great virtue, Ewan. (*He rolls on to his back and stares upwards*)

Bruce For example, Craig is currently somewhere above our heads, forty foot up in the reserves, experiencing adrenalin-pumped excitement just from huddling up in a small ball and crouching in the orange juice.

Ewan Is he?

Bruce He is.
Ewan Why?
Bruce Because he's under the impression I'm playing hide-and-seek with
   him.

Black-out

SCENE 5

The Depot

*In the darkness we hear Robbo making a strange noise like the winding-up
of an engine*

Robbo (*off, in the distance*) Arghhh-hh …

*The Lights come up hard on a small clump of Bruce, Dids and Ewan and a
damaged crate of tinned tuna steaks*

   (*Off, closer*) Arghh-hh …

   *Suddenly Robbo thunders on from one corridor and hurls a tin of tuna
   down another*

*They all watch it go. There is a pause. Bruce, Dids and Ewan look at Robbo,
who turns*

Robbo Yess. Whurr.
Bruce (*calmly*) What d'you mean, "Whurr"?
Dids What're y' playing at?
Robbo Good, eh?
Bruce (*to Ewan*) Can you check the Robbo English Dictionary under
   "Whurr", please.
Ewan "Expression of joy uttered in the delusion of having won something."
Dids He didn't win that.
Robbo I won that.
Dids I won that flaming ... clearly. Look.
Robbo Mine went tons further than yours.

Bruce, Dids and Ewan look at him. A communal sigh

Bruce The object, Robbo, of the noble sport of Shove-Tuna, is to get your
   tin of tuna in brine as close as possible to the jack, being the flan base, OK?
   Did I not make that rule absolutely clear?

Dids Well, I understood it.

Bruce Did it not strike you as at all odd that we set ours off with a gentle flick of the wrist and you had a ten metre run-up howling like a wolf-man?

Robbo Eh?

Bruce Where ours were drawing to a stop, yours was still picking up speed and had flames licking off the back?

The bell rings. They all automatically do their time-honoured fake yawn for the end of shift

Well, you can't argue that wasn't an exciting shift. We've loaded sixteen cages, played fish-fencing and been present at the launch of a tuna satellite. (*He nods*) D'you want to go and get that back off Venus, Robbo, and we'll try again tomorrow night.

Robbo doesn't go off

Dids But I won.

Bruce (*slowly, for Robbo's benefit*) Put all the damaged units in the recoup area, yeh?

Robbo goes off this time

Dids That one, I won.

Bruce (*turning*) What?

Ewan (*heading towards the corridor after Robbo's tin; passing Dids*) We saw it, Dids. Don't worry. It was a princess amongst shoves. It might even get shove of the month.

Dids looks at Ewan. Ewan moves to peer down the corridor

Bruce (*intervening*) Yeh, you won, Dids.

Dids heads for the exit, staring at Ewan: only we and Bruce see Dids' look

Ewan Did, er — did you see that tin go?

Bruce I did.

Ewan Have you seen where it's gone? Geoff Capes couldn't've thrown a tin of tuna that far.

Bruce That is a powerful man we're looking at.

Dids leaves underneath; simultaneously, Craig appears triumphantly above

Craig Stop looking!

They look up at Craig

Bruce (*mock-beaten; to Ewan*) Ewan. Stop looking.

Craig End of shift. I won! (*He jumps down*) Y'd never've got it. D'you know where I was?

Bruce I don't.

Craig The Highland Lentil packet soup.

Bruce Oh, you crafty little fox.

Craig That's right up in the fifth reserve. I've never climbed up that high before.

Bruce I know, Craig. Even the fork lifts get a bit wobbly reaching up there. Well done, mate. See y' tomorrow.

Craig Y're right up level with the catwalks when y're in the fifth reserve.

Bruce I know.

Craig It's like New York.

Bruce Well don't tell y'r mum you've been up there, Craig, or you'll have me in trouble.

Craig (*suddenly stung*) Why am I going to see my mum?

Bruce Eh?

Craig I don't see her every ... it's not all the t ... She brought me tea across *once*. It's only *Dids* says she's there all the time.

Bruce (*comfortingly*) I know.

Craig It's only him says it's all the time.

Bruce Well, don't let it get to you, mate. What you have to remember, Craig, is that today, you won hide-and-seek, and he didn't. And no-one can take that away from you.

Craig Mm.

Ewan (*shaking Craig's hand*) Well done, mate.

Craig Right.

Bruce See y'.

Craig Yeh. (*He smiles*) See y'!

Craig heads for the exit, reasonably happy with that diagnosis. Bruce and Ewan wave him off as he disappears down the row

At the point where Craig obviously disappears, Bruce and Ewan turn away immediately

Ewan No, what I'm saying is, when Robbo thundered down here howling, were you thinking what I was thinking?

Bruce What, that we should jack in working here and tour round fairgrounds with him in a cage?

Ewan That it might not've been Dids' sprout that had Glen's name on.

Bruce Mm-mm …

Ewan We might've got it wrong in our little who-dun-it.

Bruce I have to admit, I'd rather not think about that.

Ewan What?

Bruce The whole concept.

Ewan What whole concept?

Bruce The whole prospect of working side by side with a sixty horse-power body that's being operated by a one donkey-power brain.

Ewan It's not a good ratio.

Bruce Traditionally people like that end up at the age of forty smashing down doors with their foreheads bellowing "Here's Johnny".

Ewan Let's not think about it.

Bruce OK.

Ewan OK.

Bruce Just make a mental note that we must never give him any rabbits to stroke.

Ewan Done. (*He nods*) See y'.

Bruce T'ra. (*He finishes a last bit of picking*)

Ewan leaves

Craig turns up again like a faithful hound

Craig Bruce!

Bruce Craig. You know it only seems like moments since we last met.

Craig I know. Well it is. But I've just ... I was in the locker rooms, and — (*slightly nervously*) guess what I've got in my pocket.

Bruce You know — if this was a fairytale now, I'd guess correctly and you'd vanish in a puff of green smoke.

Craig Eh?

Bruce Craig, as Li Ho Ping said, "Any man who comes up to you and says 'Guess what I've got in my pocket' should never be engaged in conversation".

Craig Li Ho Ping?

Bruce Oh, yes, mate. (*He starts to push the cage away*) Ancient Chinese Philosopher. Fourth Dynasty. Dedicated his life to writing smartarse comments for the bottom of calendars.

Craig (*smiling*) Yeh?

Bruce It's his wife I always felt sorry for. Every morning: "How many Weetabix d'you want, Li Ho?" "Ah, ask not how many Weetabix I want, rather how many Weetabix you are prepared to give."

Craig (*beaming, as he digests this*) ... to give. Ha! That's brilliant.

Bruce (*clunking the cage past Craig*) I'm out of here. Craig.

Craig No, no — (*he suddenly scrabbles through his pockets*) I've got a letter.
Bruce (*moving to the exit*) Well, you lucky lad, Craig. Feed it some milk and
    it might grow into a word.
Craig It's from the little office in the sky.
Bruce (*stopping*) Is it?
Craig I just got it.

There is a slight pause

Bruce (*slightly gobsmacked*) Well, you lit-tle hero! *You* got it?
Craig What?
Bruce Don't be modest. We both know the last person to get a little letter
    from the sky is now a shift manager.
Craig I know, it was him who gave it me.
Bruce Well, let me be the first to shake you by the hand. Eh, you're a dark
    horse. I didn't even know you'd applied for the management course.
Craig No, no, it's for you. I got it for you.

Bruce looks at Craig. There is a pause

He was looking for you. I said I'd bring it. (*He hands the letter over;
nodding at it*) It's got the company thingy on.

*Bruce takes the letter in the manner of someone receiving a telegram from
the front, looks at it, then at Craig, then pauses*

Bruce It has. (*He smiles*) And as Li Ho Ping also said, "The opening of a letter
    with the company thingy on should always be done in private."
Craig Oh. Right. (*He pauses*) Yeh.

Craig doesn't want to leave. But he does

*Bruce looks at the letter. He doesn't open it. He drums his fingers on it. As
he does, music plays, carrying us into ——*

Black-out

SCENE 6

The Depot. A day later — Wednesday night

Almost before we've time to wonder what the letter said, the Lights come up and in thunders Dids, hounded by Craig. Dids is eating a bar of some description out of a sinister space-age silver wrapper

Dids Well, it's what I have for breakfast. If I had for breakfast what you have for breakfast then I'd look like you, wouldn't I?
Craig I'm just saying what they told me at the athletics club.
Dids (*wincing*) Ohh …
Craig If y' work nights, y've still got to eat a proper breakfast, even if it's at nine o'clock at night. You should eat roughage, not chocolate bars.
Dids This is not a chocolate bar. This is a "Mega-Mass Carbo Body Bar". It is a mass-building carbohydrate foodstick.
Craig Right. (*He takes this in*) And that'll make you bigger, will it?
Dids (*turning*) What?
Craig Y're eating that to make y'rself bigger?
Dids (*quietly*) If y' don't have the correct terminology, don't start the conversation, Craig.
Craig Well, I know what "bigger" means.
Dids I am eating this to increase my body's natural weight-gain potential, OK? I am eating this because body-building is an art form, Craig. An act of sculpture. Every body-builder is the sculptor of their own body and the basic fact is, if y' don't pile on some clay to start moulding about, all y've got is the wiry little frame underneath.
Craig (*innocent as ever, digesting this*) Right. (*He pauses slightly*) But it is making y' bigger?
Dids (*murderously*) It is *developing* a physique, Craig, the word is *developing*. It is an internal process. (*Pointedly*) The man who "develops" his physique (*he waves the bar*) eats high mass nutrition bars. The man who "makes himself bigger" sellotapes the boxes they come in to his chest.
Craig (*pointing, joyously*) That sounds like something Li Ho Ping might've said.
Dids (*frowning*) What?
Craig Li Ho Ping. He was a Chinese Philosopher who wrote the things for the bottom of calendars. I was thinking, can you imagine what it was like for his wife? "How many Weetabix d'you want, Li Ho?" "Ah ——"
Dids Is this one of Bruce's again?

Pause

Is this one of Bruce's little somethings-he-said that you've scrabbled round the floor after, and stuffed in y'r little cheeks like a hamster. Is it? For later?

Craig *(quietly)* No.

Dids *(smiling)* We like him, don't we, Craig? We think he's great, Bruce.

Dids pulls up Craig's sleeve to reveal a sweatband very similar to the one characteristically worn by Bruce

In bounces Bruce, with a plastic bag

Bruce Wha-hey! Don't move. *(Calling)* Ewan! This is a night you will always remember, lads.

Craig Eh?

Bruce This is a night which will be marked in calendars — *(Calling)* Ewan! — Dids, get Ewan will y'?

Dids exits obediently

Bruce They'll be celebrating it in Junior Schools, like Guy Fawkes' night. Bruce Kenny Surprise night. Where's Robbo?

Craig *(with some portent)* Is this it then?

Bruce Is what what?

Craig Y'r going on the course? Is that the surprise? Y'r going to tell them what was in that letter.

Bruce No, it ... *(Sotto voce)* Craig, let's just keep that to yourselves, that letter eh? You and me, yeh?

Craig It *wasn't* about promotion?

Bruce *(smiling)* In this world y' can have good promotion letters and bad ones, can't y'?

Craig gets the gist

Bruce *(shouting up the row)* Ewan my lord, our time slippeth away here.

Craig *(shaking his head in admiration)* Y' know anyone else'd be dead depressed.

Bruce *(back up to full octane)* This is much more important than some flaming induction course, Craig.

Ewan wanders in with a plastic coffee cup. Dids follows

Bruce *(to Craig)* You must always remember we spend twenty years of our life asleep and ten on the toilet. There is no point spending any of the remaining period depressed.

Ewan Look at that. (*He holds his cup out*)

Bruce Sit down.

Ewan Is that soup?

Bruce Never mind the soup. Where's Robbo?

Dids (*finishing his bar*) Last time I saw him he was the other end of G, frowning at a unit of shoe polish.

Ewan (*offering the cup to Craig*) Look in there.

Bruce Oh — Robbo!

Bruce exits to look for Robbo

Ewan You can see the bottom.

Bruce (*off*) Rob-bo!

Ewan They must have such a laugh planning the drinks for that vending machine.

Bruce (*further off*) Rob-bo!

Ewan They must sit around going, "How about calling this one Highland Broth?" and then all fall backwards off their chairs, laughing.

Dids Y're mad getting stuff from machines.

Ewan I know. It's like the Kremlin, that thing. Y've absolutely no idea what's going on inside and y'just have to accept whatever comes out. (*He nods at Dids' bar*) See if I was organized I'd bring a chocolate bar in, like you.

Bruce bounds back in before Dids has a chance to retort

Bruce Oh, f'r cryin' out loud. Can anyone make a noise like a female Robbo in distress?

scott, { **Ewan** Ah, can y' not introduce concepts like female Robbos while I'm eating, please.

Robbo comes down a corridor. He has a plastic bag

Robbo All right.

Craig (*nodding*) He's here.

Ewan I'll be dreaming about that all night now.

Bruce Where were you?

Robbo (*holding up his bag*) I went to the locker room.

Bruce Well never mind the locker room, I've got an unveiling. Good eh! (*He reaches in the bag*)

Robbo (*rummaging proudly in his bag*) It was to show y' something.

Bruce 'Cause I went shopping yesterday on me way home.

Robbo I went to the shops yesterday.

Bruce And I bought a little piece of silverware, oh, yes, yes, yes ——
Robbo It's silver.
Bruce Robbo. To get the old adrenalin pumping again ——
Robbo (*obviously getting something out of a box in the bag*) Well, silver
    coloured.
Bruce Robbo. Get a bit of the blood-tingle of competition going ——
Robbo (*delving into his bag*) Ready?
Bruce Shut up. Are you ready, Ladies and Gentlemen — ta-ra! (*He pulls out
    a little silver cup, more like an elongated egg-cup*)
Robbo Whurr. Good eh? (*He pulls out an enormous eighteen-inch high
    silver horn that looks like the end of a trombone, with wires dangling off
    the end*)

There is a pause as they take in the two silver objects

Bruce I have this dreadful feeling I've just been upstaged.
Dids What the hell's that?
Robbo It's for the weekend.
Bruce Extraordinary how you always feel y're getting the answer to a
    different question. (*Louder*) Why, Robbo? What happens at the weekends
    in Robbo-land?
Ewan Is it a trumpet?
Dids Y've not joined y'r silver band again, have y', Robbo?
Robbo Eh?
Bruce What silver band?
Dids He used to be in a silver band. He was telling me. He used to play the
    trombone.
Bruce Bloody hell. Did he?
Ewan Ah, the trombone. The instrument of romance.
Dids I must've seen him when I was sixteen odd if he was in Heaton Moor
    Silver Band.
Craig (*smirking*) You went to see brass bands?
Dids (*lethally*) I didn't "go to see" them, Craig. I "came out the pub" when
    they went past to try and get peanuts down the tuba.
Bruce So y're a musician, Robbo? That's brilliant, mate. What kind of stuff
    did you used to play then?
Robbo "Little Brown Jug".

Bruce waits for the other titles. There is a pause

Bruce Just "Little Brown Jug"?
Robbo I knew all the notes for "Little Brown Jug". There's only nine.
Bruce Right.

Robbo I wanted to play more, like, but the notes start getting dead hard and you have to change y'r mouth. So for the others I just stood at the back with me cheeks puffed out.

Bruce Right / well ——

Robbo But it didn't matter, like, not playing solos or being at the front. It was standing in the middle of this massive band with everyone on full whack, all playing flat out, that's just ... (*He's lost*) I love that.

Dids Hold on. Hold on. You told me that in the rehearsal room they all used to stand round you clapping and cheering.

Robbo They did.

Dids What, playing nine notes?

Robbo No, well, that wasn't for playing, like. That was 'cause if I took the mouth bit off and sucked really hard I could pick up a nectarine.

There is a reverential pause

Bruce Y're kidding.

Ewan A *nectarine*?

Robbo We could only bring in fruit for the breaks. If y' eat biscuits they come out the other end like a rabbit gun, y' know.

Bruce Robbo, if you switched the entire Coldstream Guards on to "suck" they couldn't pick up a nectarine.

Ewan A proper, big, full size / nectarine ——?

Bruce Craig, go and get one.

  Craig immediately beetles off to order

Bruce Dids, get the man a platform. Wha-hey!

Dids immediately sorts out a box of food

Robbo I can't do it now.

Bruce Course you can.

Ewan The lad's out of practice.

Robbo I mean I can't pick a nectarine up with this. This is a horn.

Bruce What, y' mean there's some kind of etiquette?

Robbo Eh?

Ewan You mean it wasn't just you? The whole band sucked fruit up?

Bruce Good God, that must've been some finale.

Robbo It's not an instrument. It's an eighteen-inch tweeter trumpet.

There is a pause

Bruce Now there's a word I've not heard for a long time.

Dids (*quietly*) He's chickening out.
Robbo No …
Dids (*quietly*) He didn't pick up a nectarine.
Robbo It's got electrics in the end, (*he waggles the wires*) hasn't it? I can't pick anything up.
Dids The end bit's the same.
Bruce Robbo mate, where exactly in your car does this go?
Robbo Where d'you think it goes? Where d'you think I'm going to put it? It goes next to the other five.
Bruce Of course.
Ewan You idiot.
Robbo It's going in the back seat.
Bruce With a rug?
Robbo In a cabinet.
Dids He's not strong enough to pick up / a ——
Robbo (*suddenly snapping*) I can pick up a nectarine, all right?
Bruce (*sensing danger here*) Steady, whoa there …

    Craig returns with a nectarine

Craig There's a crate opened already that a truck / hit ——
Bruce Give it / to ——
Robbo (*snatching the nectarine, reddening*) Give that here.
Craig All right, all right …

Robbo starts to unscrew the electrics from the trumpet end-bit

Bruce (*looking to Ewan*) OK, OK, here we go. One man. One nectarine.
Ewan (*quietly*) One donkey power.
Bruce (*quietly*) One's thoughts exactly. (*Louder*) And he's going for it!
Ewan Good old Robbo!
Bruce (*automatically using the little trophy as a mock microphone*) The first attempt to pick up garden produce with a musical instrument since Bob Beaman's radish record, set at altitude with a descant recorder. (*He realizes what he's doing with the trophy*) In fact this could make him the first recipient of the Bruce Kenny Trophy.
Ewan The what?

Dids and Craig come to look at Bruce's trophy as, in the background, Robbo prepares for the attempt

Bruce Good, eh? Only five quid. Got it from the sports shop by the swing bridge.

Ewan For what?

Bruce Games. General games trophy. I thought we could keep awarding it, y' know.

Dids It's got a picture of a squash player on.

Bruce Yes, well, funnily enough I said the competition was for made-up sports using crates of damaged food and they didn't have a picture depicting that.

There is a snort from Robbo

Craig He's starting, Bruce!

Bruce He's starting, Bruce! Come on Robbo. Go for it! …

The others let loose a volley of cheers of encouragement as an increasingly red-faced Robbo, standing on a box, attempts to levitate the nectarine with an intake of breath

All Go — go — go …!

Almost bursting a lung, Robbo sucks up the nectarine, then snatches his head back so the nectarine rests in the trumpet bell. There is a huge cheer

All Yayy!

Robbo waves his arms and there is a final bout of cheering

   During this, Debbie enters driving an electric tip truck

Bruce He's done it! Ladies and Gentlemen, the winner of — of …

They all notice Debbie apart from Robbo, still on his box

Robbo Whurr!

Bruce (*tapping Robbo's leg*) Robbo.

Robbo Mg? (*He looks down*)

There is a pause, punctuated only by the sound of a nectarine falling with a thud on the floor. All the men look at the nectarine. Then at Debbie

Debbie Y' know, it must be very comforting to know that if times ever got tough, you could always find work as an industrial hoover.

They look at Robbo, who takes the tweeter-trumpet out of his mouth

Y' see, that's the difference. If I had a talent to fall back on, there'd be none of this. No hanging around getting fobbed off with the animal shift. I'd be able to like — swoop, like a condor in the Sierra Madre, picking at anything I wanted, instead of waddling round like a duck in Heaton Park, being flaming thankful for whatever I get chucked.

Ewan looks at Bruce

God it'd be good, that, eh? You (*she nods at Robbo*) are a lucky man.

She drives out again along the other corridor

The lads watch her go, then instinctively turn to Bruce

Dids What the hell was all that about?
Craig Who's she then?
Dids Is she on this shift now?
Bruce (*seeing they're all looking at him*) Oh, well now's the time to ask isn't it, boys? For God's sake don't ask while she's here.
Ewan (*shaking his head*) I'm never sitting on a rock am I?
Dids You didn't say anything.
Bruce I was trying to follow the thing about the duck.
Ewan When I meet people for the first time, I'm never lounging coolly on a rock, looking like something out of a jeans advert. I'm always standing round cheering 'cause someone just sucked up a nectarine.
Bruce She must've been taken off days to cover for Glen.
Craig (*looking down the corridor*) She's picking errand-boy. She's coming back.
Ewan I mean that is just tragic, isn't it?
Bruce OK, why don't we make a better impression here?
Ewan Well, I thought it was tragic.
Bruce Can we just try and look a bit more casual?
Robbo (*staring at the trophy*) Is this mine then?
Craig Look what? I don't / understand, Bruce.
Bruce First impressions, all that.
Robbo Have I won this?
Bruce Forget that a bit, eh, Robbo? We'll dazzle her with the cut and thrust of our intellectual debate, OK? You lot get ready with something impressive to say. I'll — waylay her with something cool and casual.

Debbie enters, approaching the men

Craig What? I don't understand ——

Bruce (*to Craig*) Shhht.

Bruce prepares himself for something cool and casual. Then as Debbie trundles into the central area, Bruce just feints across her path. She stops. She leans over the front of the truck. Bruce smiles

Listen, y've got us all worrying about this duck thing.

Debbie Pardon?

Bruce This turning into a duck and waddling round Heaton Park. Is it something that happens a lot? Every full moon or something? Only I think contractually we've got a right to be told if we're working with a were-duck.

Debbie (*looking at him, then winking*) Don't worry about it. It was a metaphorical duck. (*She starts to move off again*)

Bruce Not a metaphorical duck? Those are the worst. I hate metaphorical ducks. We used to have a flock at the back of our house that kept ganging up and attacking our hypothetical cat.

Debbie looks at him again

I mean if it's something you want sorting out, like, y've got the best brains in the depot round y' at the moment. This is the intellectual nerve centre of the night shift. Isn't it, lads?

Debbie turns to look at the clump of Dids, Robbo and Craig. Bruce, behind her, silently urges them to say something

Dids
Ewan } (*together, almost inaudibly*) All right.

Craig (*mouthing at Bruce, wincing like a lost puppy*) I don't understand.

Robbo Is this for sucking that nectarine up?

Bruce (*sotto voce*) Ohh I'm so proud of you-oo.

Debbie Lads, are we on a break?

Bruce Eh?

Debbie (*looking at her watch*) I mean, are you doing any picking, you lot?

Bruce Course we are.

Debbie What, by telepathy?

Bruce (*smiling*) No, well, y' see, this is the difference, isn't it?

Debbie Is it?

Bruce On nights. Difference of mentality, y' know. We don't have this "New York, head down up and back down the rows" regime. We tend to operate on a more kind of ... Parisian Left-bank street-café model.

Debbie Do you now.

Bruce Oh, we do.

Debbie Well, that's probably more a difference in shift managers than mentality, actually. Day shift, this place is swarming with people in white coats and clipboards. (*She nods*) All it'd take is that catwalk up there being a monorail and the place'd look like the end of a James Bond film.

Bruce And what a tragedy that is, y'see. That's why y'r better off on the animal shift. (*He beams*)

Debbie (*leaning over the front of her truck with a wry smile*) You know, there is no sadder sound in this world than a man trying to defend his ego.

Bruce In fairness I'd wait until y've heard Robbo play "Little Brown Jug".

Debbie I have to tell you I used to go out with a bloke who worked for British Rail and his opening gambit in every conversation was, "There's a blue button at the back of every Sprinter Train and unless I push it, that train doesn't — go — anywhere".

Craig (*leaping up*) Ah, well, I hope y'r not implying it's not important, because if Bruce makes a mistake with his list, his picking list, y' know, Glossop doesn't get any Fudge! (*He beams*)

Dids Shut it, Craig.

Craig sits down

Debbie The point was if my ex worked animal shift he'd probably try and make it sound like you just did.

Bruce (*mock-indignant*) What d' you mean? It's true. (*He turns*) Look at that. (*He indicates the dubious tableau of our boys*) Just look at these people. You'd pass them by, wouldn't you? On days. Whip past on y'r truck. Never realizing what treasure troves you're looking at here. Each of these people is a Tutankhamun's tomb, you see. Behind these stone slabs there are piles of fascinating little golden twiddly bits of life history all stacked up and if you've not got time to push the slab back and stick y'r head in, y'd never find out.

Debbie I seem to remember if you break into a sealed tomb it unleashes a hideous curse on your offspring.

Dids Yeh. Your dad used to do that, didn't he, Craig?

Craig Just shut / it ——

Bruce (*sotto voce*) Thanks, lads. (*Louder*) Yes, you see Craig here is the only athlete in this country currently being taught to throw the discus by a poet.

Craig No, using one / poem for ——

Dids And his mum brings his tea across on a tray.

Craig (*quietly*) She doesn't.

Dids She comes across the road with it under a teatowel.

Bruce *Dids*, OK, this man can put a unit of Marmite on his back and still clap between press ups ——

Dids (*not looking up*) Two units.

Bruce Two units, sorry. Ewan was once interviewed on local news because the bloke in the flat below him had his pit bull terrier shot with a crossbow and Ewan said ——

Ewan } (*together*) "We're all shocked, the dog was no trouble." (*They sigh
Bruce }   *simultaneously*)

Bruce With the caption "A neighbour" underneath him. (*He turns*) And Robbo ... well, Robbo ...

Debbie I think I've seen what Robbo excels at, haven't I?

Robbo (*still looking at the trophy*) So will I get me name on this?

Bruce (*wincing almost imperceptibly*) Yeh. Well, precisely. (*He beams*) See what you miss?

Debbie looks at Bruce. Bruce's confidence makes him attractive

So what about you?

Debbie (*smiling*) OK. (*She starts to move off*) My name's Debbie Petley and I cheated on my bronze survival swimming because I touched the bottom every time I turned round. How about that?

She exits

Bruce looks after her, slightly thunderstruck

Music begins to play

There's a pause. Everyone looks at Bruce

Ewan Well, say something.

Bruce (*turning to Ewan*) Debbie Petley. (*He points, as if in wonder*) That was Debbie Petley.

Black-out

Scene 7

The Catwalk

The music fades

In the darkness we hear Bruce

Bruce No, but Ewan, you don't realize. That girl was Debbie Petley.

The Lights come up swiftly

Ewan and Bruce are on the catwalk. Bruce is looking down

Ewan I do realize that girl / is ——
Bruce That person down there is Debbie Petley.
Ewan Look, are we going for this cigarette or d'you just want to spend the rest of the break telling me ——
Bruce It's *Debbie Petley*, Ewan. You don't realize. It's like meeting—like meeting someone out of *Star Wars* for me, that is.
Ewan Eh?
Bruce Y'know, a mythological figure who played a formative role in my childhood but I never thought I'd actually meet. Have y' never had that?
Ewan Not since I met them Argonauts down the butcher's.
Bruce Ten points.

The gesture

Bruce No, Debbie Petley achieved the legendary status of having the prefix "that" put in front of her name, which as you know is the school equivalent of a knighthood.
Ewan What school?
Bruce My sister's. That Debbie Petley used to hang around with Elaine Dutton and Sarah ... someone whose name I forget but who allegedly once made love in the sick bay using a surgical glove as a contraceptive.
Ewan She didn't.
Bruce She did.
Ewan What a marvellous sight that must have been.
Bruce Elaine Dutton was the one who smoked cannabis before her GCSE French and wrote the line "Je t'adore Charles Aznavour" three hundred times. And "that" Debbie Petley (*he looks down*) was apparently once carted past our Ruth in the dinner queue after falling unconscious trying to pierce her ear with an ice cube and a compass.

Ewan (*looking down*) And they were — that was ——?

They both look down. We immediately cut to:

SCENE 8

The Depot

Debbie enters, followed by Craig

Debbie (*finding an item and ticketing it*) Yeh. It's very clever.
Craig It is, i'n't it? And the second one is: "Chin knee toe, make a bow, see it go". Those are the last positions.

Dids appears with his trolley

Craig That's what Bruce meant by poetry, y' know. Not really "poem" poem.
Debbie (*politely*) That's very good.
Craig (*beaming*) I mean it's not like Fatima Whitbread runs round going, "I must go down to the sea again."
Debbie (*lost at this*) Why, doesn't she like it?
Craig (*the beam dropping*) What?
Debbie The sea.
Craig No, it's a poem. (*He nods*) That she doesn't say. Ever.

There is a pause

Debbie (*smiling sadly*) Lovely talking to you, Craig.

She moves off down the corridor

Time for Dids to move in

Dids I've got a poem, actually, that I'm working on. It goes:
> "There was a young man called Craig,
> Who was a total nob-head.
> His friends called him nob-head,
> But that didn't matter
> 'Cause he didn't actually have any friends anyway".

Ah y' see the rhythm all goes at the end. D'y' think it'd help if I started doing discus?
Craig (*trying to come back at him*) Oh yeh, Dids, just (*he nods*) ...

Dids Just what? (*He smiles*) Come on, Craig. (*He feigns to peer, dentist-like, into Craig's mouth*) Y' must have something of Bruce's in there somewhere. (*He smiles*)

There's a pause

No? Empty? (*He heads for the exit*) Don't worry, y'll pick something up. (*He continues to look at Craig; singing gruffly*) Me ——

During the following, Dids exits

      — and my shadow.
      Walking through the Branston Pickle …

We cut back to:

SCENE 9

The Catwalk

Bruce is leaning over the railing. Ewan is trying to usher him out

Bruce No, they weren't *in* the school play, they were these three waitresses who drank all the interval wine / and—
Ewan Bruce, d'you want a cigarette this break, or shall we just go down and endure the KitKat of misery with Robbo in the locker-room?
Bruce OK. OK.

They move to exit, then Bruce stops Ewan again

  That's how they got expelled, y' know. Smoking.
Ewan I was on twenty a day in the third year. You don't get expelled for smoking.
Bruce Yeh well, (*he nods*) school like our Ruth's, where it's all "straight-jumpers-please", it's a different moral code, mate. Different principles. Plus they snook into the art block at breaktime and set all the sprinklers off.
Ewan It's not a rare name, y' know.
Bruce Seventeen papier mâché figurines had to be sent into the Examining Board retitled "porridge on a stick".
Ewan It probably isn't the same Debbie Petley.
Bruce Good if it was, though, eh, don't y'reckon? Have someone like that down here?
Ewan (*looking at Bruce*) Are we going out or not?

They leave

As they do so, the Lights cut to another entrance in the Depot

SCENE 10

The Depot

Debbie pushes her cage in, followed by Robbo. Debbie has the trophy

Debbie "The Bruce Kenny Trophy". Well that's very touching. Someone left that for posterity, did they? Or did you club together and have it engraved in memory?
Robbo (*looking up*) Yeh, I won this.
Debbie (*nodding*) Who left the trophy?
Robbo (*looking at it again*) I think it's for that nectarine.

Debbie looks at him. Not quite the answer she expected

Debbie (*pointing*) Bruce — Kenny?
Robbo (*nodding*) Bought it.
Debbie (*quieter*) If I wait ten seconds d'you think your answers'll catch up with my questions?
Robbo (*nodding*) I've got one like this at home that I won with me car stereo.
Debbie Then again there is no possible question for that answer. (*She swings nearer to him*) You won a stereo?
Robbo No, it won a competition.
Debbie *It* won?
Robbo Well, second. In Worksop.

There is a slight pause

Debbie And what happens at a car stereo competition then? Are they all lined up like Crufts and y' have to walk them round in a ring?
Robbo (*nodding*) They line up. In a field. Then the judges come and sit inside and turn it on. I only got second in the small car category 'cause I still had the back seat in, and him that won had the whole back seats taken out and he'd built a cabinet to take two, OK, two twenty-one inch sub-woofers.

There is a pause

Two.

Debbie looks at Robbo with a slight frown

So that's what I'm doing this weekend. Putting a cabinet in. But I'm adding two rows of tweeters down the middle which means I should be able to get well past one twenty-five DB, I mean just like miles past.

Debbie (*quietly*) I have this awful feeling you're talking about how loud it is, aren't you?

Craig enters

Craig Robbo, have you got my picking list, 'cause I / put ——
Debbie (*whispering to Craig*) D'you know what a DB is?
Craig A D — what?
Debbie Never mind. (*Louder*) What's a DB, Robbo?
Robbo Decibel.
Debbie (*quietly*) Oh my word.
Robbo The overall winner, the kind of overall ...
Debbie Best in show.
Robbo Yeh, he was a Range Rover, right, and he had sixteen speakers driving two thousand watts and his volume went up to ten and he put it on six, OK, and shut the doors and walked across the fields and pressed start on his remote and when it came on, it blew all his windows out.
Debbie And he was pleased about this, was he?
Robbo Everyone cheered like, and patted him on the back.
Debbie (*picking something else*) Well, that's great, Robbo. It's his mother I feel most chuffed for really.
Robbo Eh?
Debbie She'd probably given up hope of him ever achieving anything in life. I wonder if she has photos up of him on the sideboard holding trophies with broken windscreen all over his face.
Craig (*loving this*) God, that's just like Bruce.
Robbo Oh, y'r not near, the remotes go for miles. (*He produces his remote control*) Mine'd turn mine on in the car park. (*He holds the control out to Debbie*) Y' can have a go. Not through walls, like, but y' can do it off the roof.
Debbie It's OK, Robbo, better not, eh? I think legally we'd have to sound a siren so people could go into bunkers.
Craig Ha — it's dead like Bruce.
Debbie (*turning*) What?
Craig The ... what he does when he's with Ewan. Y' know, the two of them. It sounded dead Brucian.

Debbie looks at Craig for a second

Or Brucite. But that sounds like coal. Ha.

Debbie He's a bit of a legend, this Bruce bloke, isn't he?

Craig Eh?

Debbie Well, if he's got a word named after him and a prize named after him, he's not doing badly. I thought you had to be dead to have that.

Craig Well, he's not. He's around. Well, (*he looks at his watch*) if it's break now he'll be on the terrazza, but he's still ——

Debbie The what-zza?

Craig Well, they call it that, him and Ewan. It's just their place on the roof where they go to smoke 'cause you can't in the locker-room, the sprinklers ——

Debbie And so — what's (*she nods at the trophy*) Bruce do round here that's so special then?

Craig Special? (*He looks at Robbo*)

Craig Well, he's just Bruce, isn't he?

Robbo He thinks of the games.

Craig Bruce thinks of the games.

She looks at them

Black-out

SCENE 11

The Roof

It's night out here. The higher you go up, the darker it gets, it seems. This is Bruce and Ewan's secret mooching place. The skylight and fire door throw light across the area

Bruce and Ewan are lounging on a skylight in time-honoured fashion; Bruce has a cigarette

Bruce (*in the manner of a snooker commentator*) And you join us in the second frame here at Kale Moor International Arena. Clear, starlit night, warm breeze sifting gently across the rooftop making these perfect conditions for tonight's final of the Embassy World Mental Snooker Final. Don't you agree, Ewan Bennet?

Ewan D'you mind if I concentrate on this shot?

Bruce I'm only commentating.

Ewan Just give us one moment of peace, please.

There is a pause

Yes! Red into top left pocket. One point.

Bruce Clipped the black. Seven away. Free ball.

Ewan It didn't.

Bruce Look, who's the referee?

Ewan Well now there's a pertinent question.

Bruce Don't be a bad loser.

Ewan Seeing as I lost the first frame after apparently clipping the yellow ball with my break shot.

Bruce Ewan / don't be a ——

Ewan And you went on to score one-four-seven and won a Rover Metro. Pass us that fag.

They only have one, it seems. Bruce does

Bruce Wish I'd not suggested trying that blowpipe thing now. (*He sighs*) You see success isn't always a good thing. If I hadn't succeeded in hitting your cigarette packet off the ledge, the rest of those wouldn't be in the car park now.

Ewan (*contemplatively*) There was a certain joy while it lasted, though. That feeling of continuity in life. Playing the same games now that you were playing at school.

Bruce Well, people don't realize, you see, Ewan. There are plenty of company directors sleeping out there tonight who've had successful careers and climb up thinking they're getting happier — but when they look back on the bar chart of their life, they'll find the relative peak of happiness they ever achieved was that dinner hour they spent trying to kick a pencil case into someone's sports bag. Hallo?

Debbie appears on the hallowed roof terrace, carrying Robbo's remote control

Debbie All right. Not a private terrazza, this, is it?

Bruce Er, no, no. Not private. (*To Ewan*) Is it?

Debbie I didn't know you could get up here. Your little friend down there told me about it.

Bruce Big muscles little friend or big car stereo little friend?

Debbie Chin-knee-toe little friend.

Bruce (*nodding to Ewan*) *Little* little friend.

Debbie (*going to the edge of the roof*) Don't stop whatever. I just came up to try a little experiment.

Bruce Really?

Debbie Yeh, it's just a — er... (*She presses a button on the remote*)

Somewhere far away we hear a brass band start to play

Well, there y' go.

Bruce (*turning to Ewan*) Did you see that? She just pressed that button and a parade started somewhere in Stockport.

Debbie (*smiling*) And that's only on three. If it was on five it'd be up here with us.

Bruce (*to Ewan*) If that control got into the wrong hands ...

Debbie I didn't think anyone listened to brass band records. (*She turns the music off*)

Bruce That'll be Robbo's remote then?

Debbie Doesn't it bother him that the only other people looking in the same rack at the record shop are all smoking pipes?

Bruce No, well, when Robbo walks into shops most people run out, so he'd never notice.

Debbie (*getting a packet out of her pocket*) So y' sneak up here for y'r breaktime fags then?

Bruce Well, it's this or the car park. (*He throws her some matches*) There's sprinklers in the locker room.

Debbie S'OK, ta. (*She smiles*) I'm cold turkey. (*She half smiles to herself*) I had a bit of a bad experience with sprinklers.

Bruce looks at Ewan and gestures: "It's her!" Ewan does a mock-excited gesture back

(*Taking some gum from the packet and putting it in her mouth*) I've got as far as buying this nicotine gum stuff, as long as I still slope off somewhere illicit to chew it. (*She turns*)

There is a beat's pause

So you dream up all these games out here then?

Bruce Eh?

Debbie "Bruce is the one who thinks up the games." That's the word on the shop floor. (*She smiles*) Funny how I get this picture of the Oompah-Loompahs crowding round Willy Wonka to hear the latest recipe.

Bruce smiles back at this gentle jibe and rallies

Bruce Yeh, well we're just developing this new one aren't we, Ewan?

Ewan Er, yeh we are ——

Bruce Problem is it's a sprinkler-setting-off one so you can only play it up here. Bung us those matches.

Debbie Y' shouldn't play with matches.

Bruce It's safe. They play this at dinner parties.

Debbie Oh yeh? (*She throws the matches back*)
Bruce It's an ice-breaker.
Debbie What dinner parties?
Bruce Oh, you know what it's like. Peter and Jackie don't know Clive and
Jill and y've run out of conversation by the end of the salmon terrine and
suddenly the rest of the evening starts to stretch away like this desert road
with one very small gas station of conversation every sixty miles.
Debbie I don't actually.
Bruce Well, if they played this up front, none of that. It's for people who're
going to be spending a lot of time together. (*He smiles*) What you have to
do is light the match, and y' hold it. And y've got the time it takes to burn
to tell the story of your life. OK?

Debbie just looks at him, she hasn't sussed him out yet

(*Jumping up on the skylight*) I'll go first. Right. And-d … (*He strikes a
match*) Right! I was born in Stockport. And we had a doorbell that played
Clair de Lune. And I always thought that *Clair de Lune* was a girl's name.
And my mum used to tidy up for the cleaning lady, who was called Mrs
Jerrams and she was too fat to bend down and plug the hoover in. Er — and
at school I discovered you could turn on the school crossing signs with a
chip fork and I can clear thirty-four packets of Hovis cream crackers off a
standing jump — argh! (*He shakes the match out*)
Debbie (*with a wry smile*) Busy life.
Bruce See? We're practically related now. (*To Ewan*) Go on.
Ewan (*sotto voce to Bruce*) I don't really like this kind ——

But Bruce bustles Ewan up into position

Bruce Go on ——
Ewan I / don't ——
Bruce Go on. I'll light it for y'. Y' ready? Anddd — go!

*He lights a match and shoves it, Olympic torch - fashion, at Ewan, who's not
exactly as high octane as Bruce about this*

Ewan Er, well, my — er — name's Ewan ——

There is a slight pause

Bruce OK. Chapter Two?
Ewan Because my dad's dad was Scottish. So we had loads of Coldstream
Guards records but only ever played them on New Year's Eve. And the flat

we lived in was … (*he pauses*) there was a sticker of Duran Duran on the water heater. (*He pauses*) Ow. (*He waves the match out*)

Bruce Good eh?

Ewan (*dully*) Yeh.

Bruce Right! (*He chucks the matches to Debbie*) And finally.

Debbie holds the matches. Nobody makes her do anything she doesn't want to

Debbie And what if I don't want you to know my life story?

Bruce Well, it's not just for us. You know. Psychologists use this to solve deep behavioural problems.

Debbie Oh yeh?

Bruce Look at Ewan. For years no-one's been able to explain why he wakes up every New Year's Eve and sleepwalks round the bedroom playing "Her Name Is Rio" on a set of imaginary bagpipes.

Debbie Well, I don't have any problems.

Bruce What about this duck condition?

Debbie (*laughing, shaking her head*) If y' say something once round here it doesn't just disappear, does it? It gets flaming trapped and keeps coming round again like unclaimed baggage.

Bruce (*remembering an anecdote and pointing*) Y' know I saw a woman going for a piece of unclaimed baggage at Leeds Airport last summer. But it wasn't hers. And by the time she'd realized, her charm bracelet was stuck in the buckle. And it was too heavy for her to lift, and no-one helped 'cause she was tromping over their trolleys and eventually she had to just follow it and disappear through the flaps.

Debbie (*interested almost despite herself*) Really?

Bruce It must've been fabulous that. It's rather like seeing the afterlife. You always wonder what goes on through there, don't you?

Debbie Well, when I went on the school trip to Venice, the teachers said, "Don't buy any delicate souvenirs to take home, 'cause Italian airport staff jump on all the English suitcases".

Bruce They don't do they?

Debbie I think it was to stop anyone spending buckets on stuff they couldn't get back.

Bruce Right.

Debbie Good thing was, just as they finished telling us, this girl from our form burst into tears and said she'd just bought her mum a three foot long gondola made from thin strands of coloured glass.

Bruce Excellent. Did she get it home?

Debbie She got it two thousand miles. She had to have it on her knee on the plane, then carry it on the coach. Then when she got to Bramhall petrol station, her mum shut the boot on it.

Bruce When we went to Martinmere Wildfowl Reserve my best mate bought his mum a tin foil painting of a Muscovy Duck taking off, 'bout that big, (*he indicates*) and brought it home dead proud to find out that exactly that painting had been to the left of their fireplace for fifteen years.

Debbie Get lost.

Bruce He hadn't noticed.

Debbie And did they put it up?

Bruce (*nodding*) Tragically they did. On the other side of the fireplace. I went round and they had two identical ducks simultaneously taking off at the same angle. It was like sitting on some kind of aircraft carrier.

Debbie It is like a baggage carousel this, you know. We're back talking about ducks.

Bruce Well, we wouldn't be if you lit that match. The duck's all we've got. That match will illuminate the tomb of your past.

Debbie Now the tomb's back.

Bruce Y're avoiding this.

Debbie Listen. If I went through the highlights of my life while a match burned down I think there'd still be time for Barbara Dickson to give us a song in the middle.

Bruce Ah come on. Y' must've had loads. What about school?

Debbie Well, I probably did at school, but that was school, wasn't it?

Bruce So?

Debbie So it all changes.

Bruce Does it?

Debbie Course it does! They don't stay highlights — I mean this (*she nods down to the warehouse*) was a highlight. (*She can't help a laugh at this*) This place was bloody like turning up at the gates of Disneyland, coming to work here, when I started. Getting y'r pay packet. Having the kit. Working with real proper people, not Pauline and Sarah who covered their text-books with Liberty Print wallpaper.

Bruce Did they?

Debbie (*winking*) Girls' school. Solicitors' daughters. (*She gestures: "money"*) Gucci satchels.

Bruce wolf-whistles

It was only exciting 'cause everyone else was at school. 'Cause I went to the pub at lunchtime and met all the staff who were going back to teach Home Economics to girls I was sitting next to, three months before.

Bruce And it's not like that now?

Debbie What?

Bruce Disneyland?

Debbie (*smiling*) I think I'd probably call it Lard-land, actually. It's like big piles of hours stacked up like cooking lard. Y' beetle in every shift on y'r

little trolley and y' pick another little shrink-wrapped pack of eight out of
this bloody skyscraper y've got to get through. And y' dump it into this
lorry. And the tailgate shuts. And that's another eight hours y've got rid of.

*There's a slight pause. Suddenly Bruce claps his hands very much in his
typical style*

Bruce Well, thank God it's not going to be like that any more, eh?
Debbie Mm?
Bruce Eh, Ewan?

We'd forgotten about Ewan. As indeed Bruce had. Ewan looks up

Ewan Er, yeh.
Bruce Is it not the best job in the world down here?
Debbie Is it?
Bruce You are standing on the verge of a new continent here. I'm telling y'.
   Everything changes down here at night.
Debbie Does it?
Bruce Everything. It's like a different world to all that.
Debbie How come, Bruce?
Bruce 'Cause y' forget that one man's lard is another man's — stuff to spread
   on the floor to make the Bernard Matthews Crispy-Crumb Ice Hockey
   rink.
Debbie So y'r saying it's different just 'cause you play stupid games with
   food?

Bruce looks at her — with a smile of challenge

   Sorry, Bruce. I'm not going to play games with food, if that's what you
   mean.
Bruce (*with a flourish*) Games with food? Is this not Kale Moor Depot? Am
   I not Bruce Kenny? Do we just play "games with food"?

She looks at him. So does Ewan. Bruce beams

Black-out

SCENE 12

The Depot. A day later — Thursday night

From the pitch black we hear a sudden bizarre booming recorded voice, talking very dramatically. Like God

Voice The time — is eleven thirty pm. The year — is nineteen twenty-nine. The place — is Marrakesh.

Movie-soundtrack "steam-train-billowing-across-plateau" kind of music swirls in. We move from an exterior to an interior train atmosphere; a door is heard sliding open

Voice 2 (*in a bad French accent*) Messieurs et mesdames, welcome aboard ze eleven-thirty overnight train from Marrakesh to Tangiers.

The Lights come up to reveal everyone, including Debbie, sitting round, with a little flourish of speakers — a full family of Robbo's tweeter-trumpets — c, bellowing this sound out. A lead trails off through a corridor

Oh-hoh. Ladees and gentermen ...

There is the sound of a whistle

... this is Casablanca now. Casablanca first stop.

We hear the door slide open

Ho hoh. Sorry to wake you sir, but ——

There is that unmistakable sound of a cadaver slumping to the carpet accompanied by the crash of a glass

Oh *mon dieu*! *Il est mort*! He is dead!

There is a sudden "dum dugger-dum" from the orchestra

Monsieur Piers Lurcock has been stabbed through the aorta with the Moroccan Railways silver letter opener.

Another shriek of horror from the orchestra

Voice 2 No-one has got on or off! Ze murderer was in first class.

Musical flourish

Ze murderer is still on ze train!

Musical flourish

Ze murderer — is one of you!

The music bellows out in horror. And stops

Bruce nods to the frowning Robbo

Bruce Robbo?
Ewan (*suddenly*) It wasn't me.
Bruce I mean turn the stereo off.
Robbo Oh. (*He does so*)
Bruce (*eyebrows raised*) Well then.
Craig Does that French bloke know who did it?
Bruce Course he doesn't know who did it. He's just a voice to set the scene.
  Although (*he turns mysteriously*) there might be some clues in what he
  said. From now on, there's clues everywhere. (*He smiles*) All night, the air
  is going to be full of 'em. Like butterflies. (*He gets out an A4 envelope and
  grins*) The passengers. Here we go.

*Bruce fans out six fancy A4 envelopes in different colours and goes round the
group, letting each of them pick one*

Craig But who's got the clues?
Bruce You have. In each character's life story are the clues. Don't look yet.
Craig (*taking an envelope*) But how do we tell people the life stories?
Bruce Just by picking, chatting, like a normal night, Craig. Only tonight …
  the person chatting won't be Craig, will it?
Craig Won't it?
Bruce It'll be whoever's on that card.
Dids (*taking an envelope*) What if y' get a woman?
Bruce (*offering the envelopes to Debbie*) They're all unisex. You just choose
  the male name at the top.

Debbie looks at him and takes an envelope

Or the female. OK. Are y' ready? (*He looks round*)

They're all poised

Bruce Good eh? Open — sesame!

They all open up. And read. There is a moment's pause

Ha.

Dids (*quietly*) Bloody hell.

Craig (*frowning*) Eh?

Dids (*reading stiltedly*) "Father Patrick O'Rourke, the gentle Catholic missionary."

Ewan (*reading*) "Harry Houghton. The wise-cracking comedian."

Bruce Deb-ra?

Debbie (*with a wry smile; reading*) "Harriet Deville-Coutts, the spoilt Oxford undergraduate."

Bruce Ha.

Robbo "Francis Mayhew. The emotional young poet."

Bruce (*sotto voce*) Well that'll be interesting. (*He turns*) What about you, Craig?

Craig (*frowning; reading*) "Dr Damon Costello. The smouldering, sexually charismatic archaeologist."

They all look at him

Bruce Well, ladies and gentlemen. When we meet again, this will be the eleven thirty-five night train to Tangiers. And there'll be a murderer in our midst. So this is (*reading*) "Claude Heakin, the shy librarian" saying: "Would you go and read quietly, please?"

They get up with their cards and make to leave. As they do so:

Debbie Who plays this exactly?

Bruce My sister at dinner parties. But that's not a clue.

Debbie looks at the card and walks off, a wry smile on her face

Ewan (*watching Debbie, trying to smile*) So — great, so we're kind of playing this so she plays, yeh?

Bruce Eh? (*He turns*) Course we're not. It's what we're after, this, anyway, isn't it? Bit of adrenalin. But no casualties. (*He smiles*) It's combat without tears. Tension without bloodshed. (*He pauses*) Murder without sprouts. (*He beams*)

Ewan looks at Bruce

Wha-hey!

Bruce presses a button on the remote control; immediately train effects and music blare out

Black-out

ACT II

Scene 1

The Depot

The Lights come up

From one corridor, in comes Dids, with his trolley. From another corridor, in comes Craig with his. They meet for the first time in their murder mystery characters. There is a somewhat awkward moment

Craig (*finally*) Hallo.

There is another awkward pause

So, er … (*he gestures vaguely*) why were you in Marrakesh?
Dids (*immediately*) Oh this is just crap.
Craig Eh?
Dids They're just crap these kinds of things. They're crap. They never work, they're just … (*He starts picking items from the shelves*) What's bloody wrong with shove tuna? Throwing a tin of tuna to skid and — and get near something, it's got skill, OK? Sitting around with bits of paper saying "Well, you pretend to be him and you're her, and you think of a flaming proverb and you've got to draw it, and who invented penicillin ... ?" It makes me sick, all that. It makes me sodding sick.
Craig Well that doesn't sound like Father Patrick O'Rourke.
Dids Well it is, Craig. It's very religious actually, all that, 'cause it happened in the Bible, all that. When Jesus went to a dinner party and did the thing with the water and the wine and afterwards everyone said, "How about Trivial Pursuit?" and he stood up and said, "If you get that out, I'm leaving, 'cause it's crap".
Craig Sorry, who was that?
Dids (*stopping*) Eh?
Craig You were talking about "Craig". Who's this "Craig"?

There is a pause

(*Holding out his hand*) My name's Dr Damon Costello.

Dids looks at Craig and doesn't shake his hand

Craig Yes, and I've just come to Morocco after excavating the Valley of the Kings in / Egypt ——

Dids Oh shut it. Is this because we've got — whatserface — that we're playing this, eh? Not proper games? How come she's playing now? How come we ... how come ... how am I supposed to act out some Irish git building missionary huts on the banks of Lake Volta?

Craig (*nodding knowingly*) Ah, really?

Dids What d'you mean "Ah, really?"

Craig So Lake Volta's where you've been working?

Dids (*looking at Craig*) I might've known you'd play. If Bruce came up with this new game called "Let's stick forks in our eyes" you'd be the first one off to the cutlery drawer, wouldn't y'? (*He dumps some stock*) Well best of fun, Craig. (*He turns back*) No-one else is doing this, y' know? You do realize you're going to be the only person?

Ewan arrives, picking, down the other corridor

(*To Ewan*) Isn't he? (*He nods*) It's a big joke on him, all this. Like that fish fencing?

There is a slight pause. Ewan looks round, slightly dully

Ewan So what were you doing in Marrakesh?

Craig (*smiling; a little triumphant*) Hargh. Yes, well the vicar here was just telling me he's building a missionary hut on the west bank of Lake Volta. And I've just come over from Egypt.

Dids I never said west bank. I said bank.

Ewan Right.

Dids I said bank.

Ewan What were you doing in Egypt?

Craig Ah, (*he nods*) I was excavating the lost tomb of the boy king Akhen-Put-Ra.

Dids Akhen-who-what? (*He points*) See, he can't play this, he's just making it up now. You never told *me* that.

Craig You didn't ask.

Dids Eh?

Craig If you ask, you find out. That's the game.

Dids looks at Craig

It's ... in fact, Vicar, it's all a bit like archaeology. The more you dig, the more you find.

Dids (*slowly*) Or the more you dig, the dirtier everything gets and the more crap y' get on y'r hands.

Craig No, but you see, it is right 'cause we are all sealed tombs, aren't we, Vicar?

Dids I know. And if they open the tomb marked "Craig" all they're going to find is one twenty-eight metre discus badge and five thousand trays of shepherd's pie from your mum.

There is a pause

Craig (*suddenly looking to Ewan, holding his hand out*) My name's Damon Costello. Why are you in Marrakesh?

Dids (*muttering in disgust*) Ohh ——

Ewan Me? Er, cabaret. (*He nods*) I do cabaret. One month a year. At the *Fleur de Maroc* Hotel in Casablanca. So I travel round a lot. I'm — er — up and down this train line. (*He pauses*) Like a bride's nightie.

Dids What?

Ewan More tea, Vicar?

Dids I'm not even a vicar. That's him (*he nods*) cocking up again.

Ewan No, no. That's my catchphrase. "More tea, Vicar" is my catchphrase. That's what I keep saying. "More tea, Vicar".

There is a pause

If you say it enough it gets funny.

Dids (*to Ewan*) Well, you just carry on being Mister Funny Man, mate. (*He picks another item*) Best of luck. Call me when we've gone back to the proper games. (*He dumps the unit in the cage*)

Craig (*sotto voce to Ewan*) We need all six lots of clues.

Dids carries on picking during the following. Ewan watches him

(*Sotto voce*) It won't work with five. If he doesn't play that's it. Ewan?

Ewan (*suddenly*) Yes, I've heard of Dr Costello.

Craig (*whispering urgently*) There's no point, it won't work with just five.

Ewan (*tacitly gesturing "shut up"*) Wasn't it you wrote that article about excavating in the Amazon?

Craig Pardon?

Ewan About how you took your chessboard along. And every village you went into, most of the primitives would have a go at the mental challenge of playing, but there'd always be one who didn't want to try any new games and was happier jumping up and down in the river, hitting his reflection with a stick.

Dids (*stopping and turning; quietly*) I'm sorry?

Ewan (*to Craig*) Fascinating article.

Craig Yeh, I remember now. (*Innocently*) It was nineteen twenty-three ——

Dids (*to Craig*) Did it say that on the card?

Craig Eh?

Dids About someone jumping up and down in a river an' that, that was on the card was it?

Craig Er ——

Ewan You don't just stick to the card.

Dids looks at Ewan

Part of the game is being the people, isn't it? That's the mental challenge. (*He shrugs*) I mean not everyone can manage it, but that's the game.

Dids looks hard at Ewan

Craig (*innocently*) Yeh, it's like me with doing archaeology, y' know. I dig up a few pieces of pot, and then just from them, I have to imagine what the whole jug looked like.

Dids looks at Craig

Ewan Very — good — point. Very good. (*He nods to Dids*) See, Dr Costello's doing really well.

Dids (*reassessing the situation quickly*) I'm not saying I can't play this game, OK. What I'm saying is there's other people out there who it's not going to be that easy for. Who're six foot tall and rhyme with Bobbo. Who'd prefer to be playing proper games, 'cause they won't be able to cope. It's him I'm meaning. It's him I'm thinking about.

Robbo enters with a picking cage

Robbo Whurr! Good eh? (*He looks round*) So why were you lot in Marrakesh?

Ewan and Craig turn to Dids

I've just been turned down for Poet Laureate, I have. I was definitely going to get it. (*He starts to pick items from the shelves*) I had it there, and I was bloody robbed.

Ewan Really?

Robbo Robbed.

Dids See? He doesn't know what's going on. He thinks it's something like the UEFA Cup.

Craig Who robbed y'?

Robbo The panel. (*He nods*) There was hanky panky on the panel.

Dids (*quietly*) They've passed laws about humiliating creatures in public, y' know.

Ewan The panel who choose?

Robbo The panel.

Dids (*quietly*) Why don't y' just prod him with a stick and play a barrel organ.

Craig (*nodding*) This must be a clue.

Ewan Don't suppose you can remember who was on the panel?

Dids (*quietly*) What d'you think?

Robbo Sir Oscar Robberts, the Right Honourable Owen Deville-Coutts, and Undersecretary Piers Lurcock.

Ewan (*looking at Dids, eyebrows raised*) Coping so far.

Craig Piers Lurcock. The murder victim.

Ewan (*nodding to Dids*) Did y' get that?

Dids looks back at him

Robbo And you're the one does comedy shows out here?

Ewan Well in the summer I am, yeh. Then I compère the Zodiac Club in London the rest of the year, 'cause it pays well, that, y' know.

Dids (*suddenly springing out of nowhere*) Aha! No it doesn't!

Ewan Eh?

Dids (*pointing*) If y' want clues that's one for a start! (*He nods to Craig*) Did y' get that?

Ewan What clue?

Dids Y've got to be quick.

Craig Which?

Dids (*quite proudly*) Clubs do not pay well. I know someone who works in the *Grey Parrot* in Heaton Moor and he says it pays rubbish. (*He points*) Got y'.

Craig He doesn't mean "club" like the *Grey Parrot Club*.

Dids Eh?

Ewan "Club" doesn't mean that in London. They don't walk round with polystyrene trays of cockles in London clubs.

Dids looks round, burning at being put down

Craig Ha! (*He wades in*) The acts in London clubs aren't like what's left of the Bay City Rollers from twenty years ago.

Dids (*quietly*) All right.

Craig They don't have posters up in London clubs saying "Could patrons refrain from snapping their chicken carcasses while artists are performing."
Dids I said OK.
Ewan And he should know what it's like, he's been in enough.
Craig I go in loads.

Dids looks at them both, cornered. Like a rat. So he bites

Dids (*to Ewan*) So are you going to do a bit, then?
Ewan Mm?
Dids Of your routine. The act, do we get to see this comedian?

There is a slight pause

Ewan (*putting up a smile*) You're seeing him. Comedian on holiday.
Robbo (*pointing*) Has he been in your club?
Ewan Dr Costello? People come in just because it's "the club Dr Costello goes to". I last saw him there in April with this beautiful woman with long red hair and an emerald headband.

Dids looks at Craig

Craig Oh yeh. Yeh. Louise.
Dids (*sneering*) "Louise"?
Robbo (*attentively*) A what headband?
Ewan Emerald.
Dids Was in there with you? A tall beautiful woman with red hair?
Robbo (*frowning*) Red?
Dids (*pointing*) OK, that's a clue. That is a definite. 'Cause a beautiful woman wouldn't go out with someone like him for normal reasons.
Ewan You what?
Dids There's something up there.
Ewan Course she would.
Dids What, with him?
Ewan Yeh.
Dids (*shaking his head*) Oh in theory, mate. In the textbook, she would. In theory women don't bother about physical ... what a bloke looks like, 'cause (*mock-intellectual*) "the inner bloke's more important". Sorry, not in practice. That's like the highway code. It'd be nice if it happened but it doesn't.
Ewan Y're getting it wrong, Dids ——
Dids I'm no-ot.
Ewan You ar-re.

Dids Biological fact.

Ewan Biological?

Dids Women were put on this earth to do one thing, OK. They are awash, right, their bodies are bloody awash with hormones screamin' at 'em to have children. They don't have to have children in the end, they can choose not to have children, but all those hormones are still slopping round there in the blood and the spit. So when a bloke turns up, OK, male, mate, what's talking to 'em (*he taps his head*) in here is exactly what's talking to female gorillas sitting round the jungle. It's not "Well, he looks sensitive, I bet he'll give me emotional space as a woman", it's "Can this gorilla stop my kids being flaming eaten alive by (*he points*) that other gorilla over there? No? Right, I'll go with that other gorilla then."

Ewan (*nodding at Craig*) Well, that's him, isn't it?

Dids Eh?

Ewan (*nodding*) He is the other gorilla. Dr Costello is y'r pack leader. This is the bloke that everyone looks up to.

Dids Who does?

Bruce (*off*) It's Dr Costello!

Bruce enters with a picking cage

It's Dr Damon Costello, isn't it? The archaeologist. The man who brought the Montezuma head out of Bolivia from under the nose of Colonel Benito? The man who dressed as a monk and traced the Medici stallion to a Tibetan temple? The man who lost the grasp in his right hand fighting grave-robbers on the banks of the Nile?

There is a pause. Everyone looks at Craig

Craig (*finally, slightly off-hand*) Yeh, that's me.

Bruce I can't speak.

Dids Eh?

Bruce I can't — you know that thrill of adrenalin y'get when y' meet a mythological figure actually in the flesh. (*He points*) This is the man with his face on a thousand clippings.

Craig Whose?

Bruce Mine! In the periodicals room at the British Library, (*pointedly*) where — I — work, we get all the archaeology journals, and I collect all the clippings about this man. Let me shake your hand.

Robbo (*doggedly*) So why were you in Marrakesh?

Bruce (*shaking hands with Craig*) 'Cause of him. I got this British Council travel bursary out of the blue. They buy any travel tickets you want.

Craig You knew I was in this area, then?

Bruce "Did I know" ... ? I know what your favourite kind of vegetable is. Course I knew where you were. (*He looks round for Debbie*) Are we all here? Where's the sixth traveller?

Ewan She's — er — not been (*he nods*) through yet.

Bruce R-right. So — er — so, so, so ... (*he randomly points to Robbo*) what about you?

Dids (*quietly*) Oh, not all this again.

Robbo I've been trying to write this poem out here, for a bloke. Who's paying for it, like. But I can't write anything.

Bruce Why not?

Dids He started off "There was an old man from Marrakesh" and got stuck.

Robbo I can't write anything since this Poet Laureate thing.

Dids Hold on. That's a clue. Why've y' come to Africa to write a poem? Poets go to romantic places to write poems, not to three thousand miles of scorching hot wilderness.

Craig (*lounging on a pile of boxes*) Well, that's where y're wrong, Father.

Dids Or did he want it about sand, this bloke? Is he a builder?

Craig (*a bit louder, to gain everyone's attention*) Well, that's where you're wrong, y'see, Father.

Dids turns. Everyone looks at Craig

Sand dunes can be romantic. Y'see it depends if you're walking over them gasping for water or like making love in them at night.

Everyone turns fully towards Craig

Doesn't it?

Dids And you've done that, have you?

Craig Yeh, I — (*he nods*) — I brought Louise here once.

Dids (*a smile starting to form*) And you made love on the top of a dune. Bearing in mind I can't eat an orange on Morecambe beach without getting sand in it, you made love on a sand dune.

Craig No, well we went down to this jetty. Like a launch for boats thing sticking out into the river.

Dids (*smiling evilly, and nodding*) Go on.

Craig Well, that's it. That's where we — (*he nods*) went.

Dids And you looked up at the moon, but you didn't know any love poems so you had to just stroke her hair and say "Darling — chin knee toe, make a bow, see it go."

Craig No we / did make love ——

Dids And she said, "Hold on a minute. That's the kind of thing a bloke'd say whose mum brings his tea across on a tray."

Craig We had sex actually, and it lasted ages and it was damn good and / we ——

Dids (*pointing*) Harghh! (*He continues to shout though Ewan's next line*)

Ewan (*looking at Dids*) Don't worry, Doctor. It's just difficult for people to cope with sexual success in others, if they've got hang-ups about their own physical appearance.

There is a pause

Dids (*stopping his shout*) Harg-hh ...eh?

Ewan (*looking at Dids*) Well that's what you were saying earlier, wasn't it? About hormones? It sounded like the tortured mind of a man who knows his physical appearance is forming a barrier to any relationships.

Dids (*quietly*) What physical appearance?

Ewan Well, not all of it. Just one particular aspect of it.

Dids (*very quietly*) What one aspect?

Ewan (*after a pause*) The dog collar.

Bruce That's true, y'can't deny it.

Ewan I mean you can't, can you? Being a priest. (*He smiles*) Sexual frustration. Might be a clue.

Bruce It might indeed. (*He swings round like a ringmaster*) They're everywhere tonight! Wha-hey! We're cooking.

Dids (*smiling: at Ewan, quietly*) Funny man. (*He continues to stare at Ewan throughout the following*)

There's a honk, off

Debbie arrives aboard her truck as before

Bruce (*shifting into high octane*) And the sixth traveller! Another new face. Another mysterious presence in our midst about whose life story we — know — nothing. (*He rubs his hands and cackles like Vincent Price*) Whoo-ha ha harghhh ...

Debbie I thought you were supposed to be a shy librarian.

Bruce (*shifting immediately from Vincent Price into a very quiet Alan Bennett*) Well, it goes in phases, y' know.

Debbie Oh, it does, right. (*She nods*) Y' mean y're a were-librarian?

Bruce I am. Every full moon I stop going "Whoo-ha-ha-harghhhhh" and shuffle round the streets saying, (*quietly*) "I'm afraid the photocopier's jammed again."

Debbie It was always going to be a tall order for you, being shy, wasn't it?

Bruce Well, how are you on being spoilt?

Debbie Oh, we're so sharp, aren't we?

Bruce (*nodding, smiling back*) We are, we are.

Craig clears his throat and holds his hand out to Debbie

Craig (*nodding*) Dr Damon Costello.

Debbie is caught slightly off guard. Bruce is like the devil on her shoulder

Debbie (*nodding*) Right.
Craig And you are?

Debbie smile-winces at the prospect of saying this name

Debbie Er ——
Bruce Come on, dear, spit it out.
Debbie (*with her eyes closed and a slight smile of embarrassment*) Harriet
Deville-Coutts.
Bruce And what information have you to impart *re* the celebrated Dr
Costello?

Debbie looks at Bruce and gives a smile of not-being-beaten

Debbie (*pulling a dead straight face and quoting verbatim in a singsong
voice*) My father always returns with tales of Dr Costello from his club.
(*She pauses*) Apparently.
Bruce (*smiling*) Well done.
Debbie (*nodding politely*) Thank you.

Ewan, watching this, is snapped away by Dids

Dids And this is Harry Houghton, the bloody hysterically funny comedy
entertainer at that very club and y've arrived just in time for his show.
Ewan (*suddenly grimmer*) No she hasn't.
Dids (*mock-surprised*) Y' mean y'r not Harry Houghton, brackets Britain's
premier jokey-japester close-brackets?
Ewan I mean / the rules ——
Dids You are — y're not? If he says he's an entertainer and he's not, it's a
clue, isn't it?
Bruce It is.
Ewan There's nothing on the card about the act / so it's not——
Dids Ah, but we don't stick to what's just on the cards, do we? We have to
build the picture up. Like they say, the whole jug from our few broken bits
of pot.

Craig It's like I / say. I said that ——
Ewan Look — / just ——
Dids He said that. The archaeologist knows his pots. The priest is quite happy to hear a confession. You should give us a bit of patter.
Bruce (*to Ewan*) Yeh, go on. Be great.
Craig (*to Debbie*) I said that about the pot.
Debbie It's very good.
Bruce (*rubbing his hands*) Go on, Harry.

They all sit round

Ewan (*going further into his shell*) Look, just ... (*He gives a short gesture which indicates "game over", mentally brushing it all under the carpet; then quieter, with a kind of smile*) I'm on holiday.

But Dids is in for the kill

Dids This is it. We're off. "I'm on holiday, and ..."

There is a pause

Ewan And that's the end of it.
Bruce That's the end of it?
Debbie What happened to the middle of it?
Dids (*loving this*) Eh y' won't get far at the *Grey Parrot* with that one, mate, I'm telling y' .
Ewan (*wanting to change the subject; to Bruce*) So anyway you know the doctor?
Dids They'll be chanting "Bring back what's left of the Bay City Rollers."
Ewan (*grittedly*) You know Dr Costello then ... ?
Dids Oh, but London clubs are different, aren't they?
Bruce Come on, try another one.
Ewan Bruce? — er — what's y'r name?
Dids See, they don't have jokes in London clubs.
Bruce Come on, come on, I've bought me drink now.
Ewan (*trying another smile*) Well that was daft, wasn't it?
Bruce Look, I don't mind how long I stay here.
Debbie Oh God, don't drag them out.
Bruce Eh?
Debbie It's y'r own time y're wasting.
Bruce (*pointing at Debbie*) "Y're just spoiling it for everyone else."
Debbie (*pointing back at Bruce*) "Let's see if the headmaster thinks it's funny."

Bruce "If y' haven't brought y'r PE kit, then you'll have to do it in y'r underpants."

Dids Eh, y're losing them, Harry. You're losing y'r audience.

Debbie (*nodding*) Did you ever have to do PE in y'r underpants?

Bruce No. Although interestingly one kid did and it was the same kid who got lost on our first cross country and ended up phoning the school in tears from a taxi booth in Bramhall.

Dids They're chatting amongst themselves. Get in there with y'r catch-phrase.

Bruce A what-what? He's got a catchphrase?

Ewan No / I haven't ——

Debbie A catchphrase?

Bruce Well, what is it?

Dids is motoring

Dids It's "More tea, Vicar."

Ewan Look, I'm the compère. I'm not the act, OK—

Dids And that's how y' compère, is it? Sulking at the side of the stage?

Ewan I'm not / sulking ——

Dids (*dead glumly*) "'Fraid next on it's the dancers." Must be a downer on the evening ——

Ewan *Look, I didn't bring my book with me, OK? The jokes are in a book and I didn't bring the bloody book, OK?*

There is a pause

    (*Quieter*) I forgot it.

There is another pause

Robbo (*to Debbie*) So why were you in Marrakesh?

Black-out

From the darkness comes a sudden volley of sound effects of a train and a whistle

SCENE 2

The Depot

The train and whistle effects end

Blackness. All are on stage except Robbo. Ewan is separate from the others, watching. Bruce sets the eerie scene with a torch

Bruce   Outside, all was darkness. But the corridors were brightly lit with torchlights. Deep in the catacombs of the pyramid, Dr Costello had finally found the lost third passage to the burial chamber. (*He nods to Craig*) Well done.
Craig   Ta.
Bruce   The search party were approaching the sealed door at the end, when suddenly there was a huge flurry of dust, the scream of four thousand years, and a hideous ghostly figure emerged out of the ether and thundered past them on the back of a mighty, snorting camel. (*He points dramatically*)

Robbo emerges aboard the truck with a J-cloth on his head like Lawrence of Arabia

Robbo   All right.
Bruce   (*ploughing on*) Cheers, Robbo. It filled the Egyptians with naked terror and thundered off into the ethereal void.
Robbo   Right.
Bruce   (*pointing*) Well, thunder off into the ethereal void.
Robbo   I'll park it by the Ryvitas.

He drives off

Bruce swings round and turns on the main lights

Bruce   (*quietly*) Cheers, Robbo. Thanks for setting the scene so perfectly. (*Louder*) Now the Egyptian guides thought this was the phantom camel-rider of Luxor.
Debbie   What, as opposed to a six-foot bloke from Bootle with a J-cloth on his head?
Bruce   It looked like a phantom camel rider if you use your imagination.
Debbie   And was the rider a phantom, or just a normal bloke who rode phantom camels?
Bruce   They were both phantoms, thank you so much, which is why all the Egyptians ran off, which is why only Dr Costello found the empty

burial chamber with the Arabian daggers on the floor. Leading him to conclude ——

Robbo enters, heading across the central area

Robbo It's by the Ryvitas.

He exits

Bruce Cheers, Robbo. To conclude: Arabs had raided the tomb and possibly buried the treasure during the Moroccan invasion.
Debbie In the mountain caves of Foum-el-Hassan. (*She nods*) That's one of my bits.
Bruce Wha-hey! Let's have it. The whats?
Debbie Cliff caves. Local tribes built ladders five hundred feet up sheer rock faces to reach them, and then secured the contents by burning the ladders.
Craig How d'you know about that?
Debbie Because I was in the British Library studying the lost idol of Akhen-Put-Ra for my Anthropology degree. (*Gathering speed*) Which is why my father, who is Heritage Secretary, arranged a summer job accompanying Piers Lurcock on a cultural exchange to Morocco.
Bruce Whoa there, Neddy! Save some for pudding, per-lease!
Debbie Now what?
Bruce Y're supposed to drop things gently into the conversation, not sloosh out the whole lot in one bucketful.
Debbie Little tip. My gran always said, "The man who uses his mouth more than his ears learns nothing."
Bruce Well, what a woman. All my gran ever said was, "I can't eat Brazil nuts, George."
Robbo (*pointing*) You were in the British Library?
Debbie I was. In fact that is when I saw the shy librarian trying to kill someone.
Craig (*pointing to Bruce*) Him?
Bruce Me?
Craig (*pointing*) Trying to kill someone?
Debbie They had to call the police to drag him off. He had another bloke pinned to the bookcase and his eyes were bulging out and he was screaming.
Craig Screaming what?
Bruce "Due back on the sixteenth means due back on the sixteenth."
Debbie He wasn't, he's making that up. He was shouting, "No-one insults Dr Costello."
Craig (*smiling*) R-right. Yes, well (*he nods*) they don't. So what was this idol, go on.

Debbie The legendary idol of Akhen-Put-Ra was a solid silver life-size model, with two emeralds for eyes because the boy king had green eyes in real life.

Bruce (*quietly smirking*) Tell you what, why don't you just photocopy the card for him?

Debbie Look, there's only you doing *Crimewatch* reconstructions, y' know.

Dids (*pointing at Craig*) And he worked out where Arabs put this green-eyed whatsit?

Craig (*turning*) Yeh, well y' see archaeology is like / putting ——

Dids How?

Craig — putting a jug togeth — mm?

Dids How d'you do that?

Craig Well, it was the daggers.

Dids Was it?

Craig Defending the daggers. D'you want to know how?

Bruce (*happy to go along with the new tack; pointing*) "Do we want to know how?" You ask us do we want to know the tragic events that deprived our greatest archaeologist of the ability to open his own bottles of Tizer?

Dids You had a fight?

Bruce Tell away.

Craig What happened was someone nearly ran off with them.

Dids You weren't guarding them properly then.

Craig Well it ... I ... it was when I was with Louise, actually. So I was distracted. I'd put them in the car on the top of the sand dune. Before we'd run down to the boat jetty.

Bruce Right.

Craig Yes. And we were lying there, because I can remember ... I didn't hear anyone at first, 'cause the wood was slatted, you know? If you looked down you could see the water underneath, on the stones. Making this patting noise. And that's all you heard. And also, also because I knew we'd end up (*he nods, finally getting the word out*) getting intimate, I'd come prepared.

Debbie What, y'd got some flowers?

Craig No, I'd brought a torch.

Debbie God, you know how to charm a girl.

Craig I mean, not a kind of hand-held Duracell one. (*He nods*) A flame one.

Debbie Thank God for that.

Craig So there was that flicking and crackling as well so I didn't hear the voices to start off. Up near the car. But I knew. Soon as I heard, I knew what they were doing, 'cause I understand Egyptian. And I heard them say, "This is the car of Dr Costello." And I thought, "They're going to get the daggers." So what happened, I ran up the sand dune. And that's hard, running up sand dunes is the hardest thing you can do with y'r legs. And I could see they'd taken the box, these two Egyptian blokes. But I knew they couldn't move fast 'cause they were heavy, these daggers. They were like … they were heavy as … (*he looks round*) hold on. (*He seizes a unit of Fudge bars*) About as heavy as this. Which is quite heavy. But, they were going down the dune, so they could skid down. And I knew if they got to their camels, I'd had it.

Debbie They'd got getaway camels?

Craig On the road.

Bruce (*nodding to Debbie*) It was planned.

Craig And so as I passed the car, I snatched up this … this hubcap, OK, off the wheel on the back and fortunately, all right, I'd done discus training.

Dids (*sotto voce*) Ohh.

Craig So coming down the slope I could turn my run into the last stage of a discus throw. And I sent the hubcap going which hit one of them. And he fell, and the daggers went … like, whack! (*He spills the box. Fudge fingers skid across the floor out of their boxes of twenty-four*) … like that, everywhere in the sand so the other bloke grabbed one. And I rolled down the dune so I could snatch one out of the sand like this … (*He demonstrates*)

Bruce He's very good.

Debbie There's Russian gymnasts who can't do that and pick up a finger of Fudge.

Bruce smiles

Craig And the other bloke got one. (*To Bruce*) Get one, get one … (*To the others*) And I turned — (*he nods to Bruce*) get one ——

Debbie He means you.

Bruce Sorry … (*Smiling, he picks up a Fudge dagger*)

Craig — and he came at me, but I stopped him, I stopped his hand as he lunged … (*he nods to Bruce*) lunge — and what happened was …

Bruce Where?

Craig There! (*He instantly arranges the lunge*) And what happened was — there was this moment, with his hand there, when we just stood … just stood in the sand, and we just looked into each others' eyes. And he — just …It was like deep, right at the back of the eyes, something was telling him … don't take him on.

There is a pause

And he backed off. He just — just nodded. And walked — away.

There is a strange moment of stillness as they find themselves caught in the picture, looking where the imaginary Egyptian walked away

Bruce You forget to say how you lost the grip in your right hand.

Debbie He shut the boot on it putting the box back.

Bruce (*pointing*) Ten points.
Debbie Thank you. Is that good?
Bruce Eighty and you get a toaster.
Debbie How exciting.
Dids Well how come if that's all true, then, that I've heard (*he nods*) he's a
   failure.

They all look at Dids

Bruce (*in mock horror*) A failure? This man?
Debbie The last bloke to say that got throttled in the British Library.
Bruce He did.
Debbie By him.
Bruce By me.

The silent Ewan watches this banter

Dids I heard someone in this carriage telling someone else in this carriage
   there was a journalist travelling in disguise under a false name on the train
   who was going to expose Dr Costello when he got back to London for being
   a right flop of an archaeologist, 'cause whatever it was he was looking for
   in Morocco wasn't there. He'd got all his clues wrong. (*Relishing this, he
   moves his pointing finger round as if he were a witch in* Macbeth) See,
   we're all here agreeing he's fantastic. But one of us is lying. (*He laughs a
   typical Dids laugh*)

Then, quietly, out of nowhere:

Ewan You could kill, couldn't y'?
Dids Eh?
Ewan 'Cause you can't stand this. (*He looks at Dids*) Can y'?
Dids What?
Ewan That he's a hero and you're not. It really hurts, that. Really makes you
   burn.
Dids (*after a slight pause*) I'm telling the truth.
Ewan 'Cause if there's something you've not got and someone else has, you
   have to go out and bite at the ankles, don't y'? Nibble away at the shins.
Dids (*quietly*) You what?
Bruce (*sensing the game getting lost here*) O — K then.
Ewan Because if y're never going to be big, the next best thing is make
   everything else smaller.
Bruce OK, lads.
Dids (*quietly*) And so who are you talking to?

Bruce Dids …
Ewan You.
Dids (*quietly*) Which bloody one?
Ewan Those are the kind of people who commit murders.
Dids I'm telling you, it'd better be the priest.
Bruce (*trying to round things up*) Okey dokey.
Dids 'Cause that's who was talking, that's the truth, so why are y'giving me all this?
Bruce Ewan ——
Ewan (*shrugging*) I'm only building up me jug.
Dids *It was the last thing I had to say on me card* ——
Bruce (*suddenly clapping his hands like a children's entertainer at a party*) So that was your last clue, was it?
Dids Yes. On me card.
Bruce (*buoyantly*) And everyone's the same? All got rid of all y'r clues, yeh?
Craig Er ——
Robbo Yeh.
Bruce Great! So we're all ready to go away and put 'em all together and work out who-dun-it? (*He turns round to them all as the Gamesmaster supreme*) Wha-hey! Good eh? OK, ladies and gentlemen. Bruce says … return to normal human beings! (*He unfurls his arm with some pomp*) Shazam! (*And clicks his fingers*)

There is an immediate Black-out, but no train sound this time, just sinister music. This carries us immediately into ——

SCENE 3

The Catwalk

Bruce and Debbie are standing where Bruce and Ewan were earlier, in a similar position, looking down into the depot

The Lights come up and the music stops

Bruce Just look at that. Look at that scene of action down there. Not a muscle stirs, but those men are moving at ninety miles an hour.
Debbie (*looking down*) Are they?
Bruce "Are they?" Those may look like stationary vehicles. But mentally that is a scene from the RAC Lombard rally.
Debbie D'you think so?
Bruce "Do I think so?"

Debbie D'you have to put everything I ask in inverted commas and shout it back at me?

Bruce "Do I have to put / everything you ask——"

Debbie Is this going to be the next thing down here, then? Doing that? Is this how y'r little catchphrases start?

Bruce "Is this how / our little catchphrases—"

Debbie (*pointing*) You know, there's a circle of Hell reserved for people who talk in catchphrases.

Bruce (*pointing back*) Did a previously timid man not just roll across the floor to seize a finger of Fudge like Tarzan going for a crocodile? Would he do that if he was anything but totally blown away by this game? It was like "Raiders of the Lost Twix" down there for a minute. Oh, no, it's opened the floodgates this. It's a new era in this depot. Wha-hey! It's the dawn of a new age! This is what Columbus must've felt like when he discovered America.

Debbie (*looking at Bruce*) What are you like?

Cut to:

SCENE 4

The Depot

The Lights come up on Ewan, Dids, Robbo and Craig in a clump. The atmosphere is as though a parade has just passed. There is a stillness

Dids is looking at Ewan

Robbo (*finally*) I can't do it.

Dids (*turning to him, from Ewan*) Well y' have to look everywhere, don't y' Robbo? There's clues everywhere.

Craig Yeh. You see, it's like a jug and / you have ——

Dids (*quietly*) Shut up, Craig. (*He looks back at Ewan*) Like over there. (*He nods*) Y' see funny men are funny even when they're on holiday. They're funny on trains. In the bath. You stick 'em on a chair in the middle of a field and they're funny. It's like being French. You can't do anything about it, you just are — it.

Craig Sorry, who's Craig? I / don't ——

Dids (*ignoring Craig totally*) Except them that were like only funny men 'cause they had someone else with them. And like when they're on their own they just go *pffftt* and saggy like an old football. End up doing pantomimes in Minehead. And I was just wondering. If it used to be "Harry Houghton and somebody else". You know. Perhaps that's a clue.

Robbo (*shaking his head*) I can't do it.
Dids I mean, might not be a clue. (*He shrugs*) He might not've killed his partner.
Craig You said Craig, Dids.
Dids Might he?
Craig Father, sorry.
Dids Y' know his partner might've (*he shrugs*) found someone else, say.
Craig There's no-one called ——
Dids Someone new. 'Cause that does happen sometimes, in showbiz. Someone new turns up who's like more interesting / and ——
Craig — no-one called Craig ——
Dids Craig, shut y'r gob and pick y'r mess up.

There is a pause. Craig looks at Dids

Robbo (*standing*) I can't—do it.
Dids (*turning*) Don't worry, Robbo. Y' don't want to get worked up. Didn't mean anything, all that.
Craig Well, the jug did. That thing about the jug / that I ——
Robbo (*through gritted teeth*) I can't.
Dids And anyway, it's finished. Forget it.
Craig No it hasn't.
Robbo (*heading for the exit, wincing: to himself*) Can't bloody ——
Craig It's not finished until it's solved, / and ——
Dids Craig. (*He stands*) Chin knee toe, shut your gob, sort your mess.

And Dids leaves with his cage

Craig looks at the Fudge bars. He winces and starts to pick them up

Craig But it's not, is it? Ewan? Over till it's solved. And we haven't done that. (*He continues picking up the Fudge bars*)

Ewan doesn't move

Until the card's read out at the end. Until then it's the same. It stays the same, doesn't it? (*He looks up*) Eh? Harry? I mean you're still Harry Houghton ——
Ewan (*quietly*) Craig ——
Craig Still Harry Houghton the comedian until / the ——
Ewan (*standing*) Shut it, Craig.

And he leaves

Craig watches Ewan go

Craig (*to himself*) It is. (*He scuffles the rest of the Fudge bars into the box*) I'm telling y'. It's the rules. (*He puts the last one in*) It's the rules.

Music

   Craig exits with his Fudge bars

Black-out

SCENE 5

The Roof

The Lights come up and the music fades

The roof is in the same half-light as before. Debbie, with her anti-smoking gum, stands quietly to one side. Bruce bounds on ebulliently

Bruce OK then, Lewis, let's just see what we've got here. The victim, unspecified age, Caucasian male, stabbed through the aorta sometime between Marrakesh and Casablanca.

Debbie watches Bruce's performance with a wry smile

   Motives, motives, motives. Well. We have firstly a disenchanted poet, just turned down for a job. We have a heroic archaeologist who's a black belt in Liho Ping, the ancient Chinese martial art of chocolate-combat. How are we doing? (*He lights a cigarette*) We also have a slightly aggressive priest, and the world's most deadpan comedian. (*He throws Debbie the pack*) Have a ciggy, you can't be a detective chewing gum. (*He acts it up, continuing*) R-right, so that means—everyone has some kind of weakness. Ha hargh.
Debbie (*looking at him, dead casual*) D'you know what mine is?
Bruce Go on.
Debbie I have a tendency to end up at three in the morning on the roof of depots playing games like this.
Bruce What? (*He turns, mock-affronted*) Y're a dab-hand? You had us on y' never played and y're a dab-hand?
Debbie (*smiling*) I had a couple of mates at school who were a lot like you, y' know.
Bruce Yeh?
Debbie I had a couple of mates who'd say things like "'Course we can pierce our ears without anaesthetic, Deb, they only use ice cubes if y' have it done

professionally you know." That was a belting game. I remember that one. (*She looks at Bruce's matches*) "Course we can smoke in here, Deb, them sprinklers are only for show, y' know, there's nothing in 'em." That was a cracker of a game, that was.

Bruce Well, would you like to just shake my hand then?

Debbie (*looking over*) Why?

Bruce Why? She sits there. Yesterday, it was dead lard. Today it's like school again down there and she says "why?" (*He stands like a king of a little kingdom*) This is the secret kingdom into which you have been drawn, missis. This is the Narnia of Stockport. You are now in the grotto of the never-ending dinner break. (*Somewhat expansively*) Down there lies an uninterrupted playtime with no bell at the end of it.

Debbie smiles as if watching a kid on the swings

And happy the man for whom the end of dinner bell never tolls! Wha-hey! Good eh? (*He beams at her*)

Debbie (*smiling, and shaking her head at Bruce*) And this is why it's all different on the animal shift, is it Bruce?

Bruce (*looking down, mid-proclamation*) You don't like the game?

Debbie Oh, I like the game.

Bruce It's a great game, this.

Debbie It is a *great* game, Bruce.

Bruce It's a brilliant laugh. I defy you to say y've ever had this much of a laugh on the day shift.

Debbie I haven't, no.

Bruce So?

Debbie So ... (*She shrugs and smiles*) It's still the animal shift. It's got a bit of a sparkler stuck in it, but it's still picking food, isn't it? It'll still be that if you get a load of maintenance brushes and punt y'rselves up and down standing in the cages like gondoliers.

There is a short pause

Bruce It's not a bad idea that, actually.

Debbie shakes her head

We could have races.

Debbie Bruce ——

Bruce In fact it's a brilliant ... y'see, that's ... you're just going to be fantastic at thinking up / games ——

Debbie Come here, Bruce Kenny.

Bruce (*after a slight pause*) Am I going to get told off?

Debbie (*smiling; she does like this bloke*) I want to try a little experiment. (*She beckons Bruce to the edge of the roof*)

Bruce (*moving to the edge*) Y're not going to start another parade are y'? They're still clearing up after the last one.

Debbie Just — (*she nods*) look at that. (*She stands behind him*) What's that?

Bruce Stockport.

Debbie When y'r working in this depot, d'you ever wonder what's going on out there?

Bruce I take it you do.

Debbie Yeh, I do, I do spend quite a bit of time thinking about people out there, actually.

Bruce Anyone in particular?

Debbie Oh, the girls in my year mainly. From school, y' know. 'Cause they're all out there somewhere. 'Cause they all did the bit with the Laura Ashley-covered text-books at school, (*she prods Bruce*) while I was in the grotto of the never-ending dinner break.

Bruce (*quietly*) Wha-hey!

Debbie (*looking at him*) It's not "wha-hey", Bruce. It stops being "wha-hey" when y' start to get this feeling that somehow y've taken part in a whopping great game show, where everyone else went home with dinghies and Rover Metros, and you only got enough points for the plastic salad tossers.

Bruce (*looking out*) S'not a bad prize, salad tossers.

Debbie It's the crap prize.

Bruce If it was the top prize y'd be dead chuffed.

Debbie But it's not, is it?

Bruce Y'd be running home shouting "Salad tossers! Wha-hey!"

Debbie But it's not, is it?

Bruce looks at her

And you can't pretend to be pleased with the crap prizes.

Bruce (*smiling, sparring*) Can't y'?

Debbie Well, y'r head can pretend, Bruce. Y'r brain's clever, it can do that. Y'r heart is very, very stupid. And it can't pretend anything to save its life. So you end up just standing there trying to pretend it's fantastic when you are, when actually you really know there's something three hundred times nicer over the hill. (*She smiles*) And there is, Bruce. There is something nicer over the hill.

Bruce (*looking out*) Buxton.

Debbie (*sighing and smiling*) Yeh. OK, Buxton. And if y'r in Stockport, and y' want to be in Buxton … (*She shrugs*)

There is a slight pause

Bruce (*smiling*) It's not that nice, Buxton, y' know. They have terrible parking problems.
Debbie Stop it, Bruce.

Pause

Bruce Why d'you want to go to Buxton?
Debbie Bruce ——
Bruce You know ninety percent of people in Buxton want to be in Glossop?
Debbie Y've been turned down for promotion, haven't you?

There is a pause. Debbie smiles knowingly

Bruce Where did that come from?
Debbie You applied for the course and got the little letter saying sorry, didn't you?
Bruce What makes y' think that?
Debbie (*smiling in the way Bruce does*) "The air is full of clues. They're everywhere. Like butterflies."

No-one's ever really spoken Bruce's words in vain, even affectionately, like this. It's a bit odd

Bruce Where?
Debbie My ex got turned down for promotion as well, y' see. That's when the stories of the little blue button on the sprinter train started. He gave it all this, like you. Trying to convince me it was this fantastic exciting job. And all the time he was trying to tell me, I knew he was trying to tell himself. And it was heartbreaking. So don't do it, eh?

There is a slight pause

Bruce What?
Debbie Come on. It does sound a bit like you going "This is the Narnia of Stockport" doesn't it, if we're honest? (*She nods down*) All this — playing games, and "that makes it all different down here and it's brilliant and y've got to play, Deb —" (*She smiles*) Why did I "have to play"?
Bruce Be / cause ——
Debbie (*almost sadly*) Because you're just trying to convince y' rself you didn't want the place by trying to convince me I didn't want the place.
Bruce You did want the place? You applied for it?
Debbie (*smiling*) Ah, now come on. Now you must've picked up some of my clues. I mean — mine were fairly big butterflies. In fact, I think some of them probably qualify as bats.

Bruce (*shaking his head, lost*) When?

Debbie Well, let's see. How about the first thing I said. The absolute first thing I said when I came in here. That was a fairly clear one. (*She raises her eyebrows* — *"No?"*) It had a beak.

Bruce The duck?

Debbie You don't normally describe yourself in terms of a duck if y'r chuffed with life, do y'? I mean "proud as a duck", you don't hear that often.

Bruce You don't.

Debbie (*winking*) This is what I got chucked. When I didn't get the place on the management induction course. They suggested I was so close it would be a great idea to just broaden my experience base. Say, by covering this new vacancy on the animal shift. So off I waddled down here.

Bruce You didn't want to do it?

Debbie Course I didn't.

Bruce (*lost*) And you still said yes?

Debbie (*frowning, her tone hardening a bit*) You don't just look at the three yards in front of you Bruce, and what they're going to be like. You have to look miles in front.

Bruce Do you?

Debbie You — yes — you have to look at (*she nods*) at Buxton, not Stockport. Otherwise you don't budge.

Bruce You want to budge?

Debbie Everyone wants to budge — course I do. If waddling around down here right now means I earn enough points to become a condor in the Sierra Madre next year, then you bloody do it, don't you?

Bruce Do you?

Debbie (*leaning in as if trying to explain to a child*) It's got to stop sometime, Bruce. You can't pretend forever down here. It's going to have to stop sometime.

Ewan (*off*) Bruce? Bruce, y' didn't say you were coming up, I was look——

Ewan emerges on to the roof, as Debbie emerged in ACT I

Bruce It's all different being a shift manager, you know. They can't sit in that office playing ping-pong with a Malteser and two clipboards.

Ewan (*quietly*) I was looking for y'.

Debbie Stop it.

Bruce turns to Ewan

Ewan Not a private ... this, is it?

Bruce What's the matter?

Ewan looks at the scene

Ewan?

Ewan (*looking at Bruce; quite brusquely*) There's trouble with Robbo. (*He throws an object into the middle of the roof. It lands with a clonk*)

Ominous music begins

We just found that in aisle C.

They all look at the object. A hard green ominous-looking thing. It's a frozen sprout

Ewan There's frozen sprouts in the warehouse.

"Dum dugger dum" goes the music; then there is a big swirl of music

Black-out

SCENE 6

The Depot

The Lights come up. The sinister music continues

There is a frozen sprout on the floor

Dids emerges carrying a flan base shield, like something out of "Alien". He fears for his life

Dids Robbo!? Rob-bo? (*He glances across the room and sees the frozen sprout. He looks up and around like a commando. In a loud whisper*) Another one! Aisle F!

Bruce and Ewan enter and gather round the sprout, as if it is a dead body. Debbie enters and watches the others, eating a finger of Fudge, somewhat less concerned. The music fades

Bruce How many's that?

They each produce a small handful of sprouts

Oh what's he bloody ... (*To Dids*) *What* did he say? He went off saying exactly what?
Dids That he couldn't do it.
Bruce In a calm resigned kind of way or a loud shouting kind of way?

Dids Like a bear that's been prodded a lot.

Bruce Oh great.

Dids I was right, wasn't I? He's gone back to the only game he's any good at.

Bruce Oh g-reat.

Dids I said he wouldn't cope with it, didn't I?

Debbie What's the flap? He's got a sprout?

Dids He's got a bag of sprouts that's been in the twenty-five degree chill chamber for three months. He's effectively got twenty nuggets of Kryptonite.

Debbie Is that a problem?

Ewan Look, you don't understand, don't worry.

Debbie You can't hurt anyone with a sprout.

Ewan You can if y're a sixty horse-power body being operated by a one donkey-power brain.

Debbie Well, yeh, but Robbo's not that, is he?

Ewan Look, have you spoken to him? We know this bloke.

Debbie How come he's building his own car stereo then?

Ewan Look ——

Bruce What?

Debbie Well, seeing's we're working out clues. We've got a bloke here who can build a car stereo, listens to it at a volume that we can hear on the roof, doesn't give the answers to the questions you ask and has a tendency to talk louder than anyone else. I reckon if y' put that lot in the computer I reckon it's more likely to shout "Y'r going deaf, mate".

Bruce (*quietly*) Deaf?

Ewan Look, we know Robbo, OK. A hundred years ago Robbo would've been locked in a room at the top of a staircase and fed bacon rind.

Suddenly Robbo bursts out from the stacks of food like a wolf man

Robbo *Whurr!*

The others jump slightly

Bruce *Robbo, don't! Put them down!*

Robbo Eh?

Bruce (*shouting*) *Drop the sprouts.*

Robbo (*pointing at Bruce with unparalleled jubilation*) *It was you!*

Bruce Eh?

Robbo *You killed him!* (*Joyously*) In the Zodiac Club this comedian (*he points to Ewan*) overheard your dad (*Debbie*) being blackmailed by Piers Lurcock, who knew your dad fixed it for his brother to get the job of Poet

Laureate. Your dad had to think of a way to get rid of him. And you saw him (*he points at Bruce*) nearly kill someone who insulted Dr Costello in the library. So your dad got a travel bursary sent to him (*Bruce*), 'cause he was in charge of giving those out. He (*Bruce*) chose to go to Morocco to meet Dr Costello. Your dad sent Piers Lurcock to Morocco on business with you (*Debbie*) as his assistant. You knew what trains he'd (*Bruce*) be taking, so you arranged for you all to be on the same one. Then he (*Dids*) heard you (*Debbie*) telling him (*Bruce*) that Lurcock was a journalist going back to rubbish Costello for being a failure. So you (*Bruce*) went a bit (*he taps his head*) crackers, and then I couldn't make it work if you'd (*Bruce*) *planned* to murder him, but I played the tape again in me car again and the first time I didn't hear that bit about the first-class Moroccan Railways silver letter-opener. Which meant if he used that it *wasn't* planned and it *does* work and *you killed him!* (*He points jubilantly at Bruce*)

There is a moment's pause. They all look at Robbo

Robbo Do I get the trophy?

They continue to stare at him

Dids (*to Ewan*) Well, well.
Bruce Robbo, did / working ——
Robbo Where's the answer card?
Bruce Later, mate. Did working all that out involve a reconstruction using frozen sprouts at all?
Robbo Eh?
Bruce Course it didn't. It's Craig. He's started playing it again. I'll kill him.
Debbie Playing?
Bruce I'll kill him. Can we split up and find him before someone gets hurt. Robbo, we're look ... (*louder*) we're looking for Craig.
Robbo Why?
Bruce He's brought frozen sprouts into the depot.
Robbo OK. I'll look down aisle A to E.

Robbo exits

Bruce (*quietly*) Extraordinary. Debbie, sorry, can you just look down F to K.
Debbie What games d'you play with a frozen sprout?
Bruce Don't worry. Just — if you see him, call me. Don't — approach.

Debbie exits

Dids and Ewan you (*he points*) go down there, look down L to Z. I've a feeling I know where he might be, the little berk.

Bruce scoots off

Dids Well well. She's picking things up pretty quick round here, isn't she? S'what happens when y' get someone new turning up.

Ewan looks off in the direction taken by Debbie

And the good thing is how her and Bruce have hit it off, isn't it?

Ewan heads for the exit

Lovely when two people click like that. Y' know, I think she'll be in on all the games, now. I bet that's her here for good.

Dids smiles and leaves. We hear him singing quietly, off, in a gruff monotone, every word intended to wound

> Me. And my shadow.
> Walking through the Branston Pickle …

Music plays, quietly at first, becoming louder during the following

Ewan looks down at the sprout on the floor as though it were a live grenade. He picks it up

Ewan (*finally*) Well, we'll have to show her the games then. (*He quietens*) If she's staying then she'll have to — we'll have to show her sprout tag. (*Quieter still*) We'll just have to show her. (*He looks at the sprout. He throws it up a little way and catches it*)

Ewan exits, in a different direction to that taken by Dids

Big, eerie music

Black-out

SCENE 7

The Fifth Reserve and Catwalk

The Lights come up

For the first and only time, we see the highest reserve. It is about six feet away from the catwalk and there is the suggestion of a sixty foot drop below

Craig is sitting hidden among the boxes, ferretting about in them

The eerie music continues. There is a criss-cross of calls from Dids, Debbie, Robbo and Ewan around the depot

Bruce enters along the catwalk

Bruce Craig? (*Louder*) Cra-ig? (*He sees Craig*) Craig?

Craig starts up; the music snaps off

Craig It's not ready. I'm not ready to start. Y'll have to go back down.
Bruce What the hell are you doing?
Craig Go back. I can't come down yet.

There is a pause

Craig resumes fiddling with something we can't see amongst the packet soup boxes

Bruce Will you get out. *We don't play sprout tag any more, remember?* It's banned. And even if we did, you can't just start playing (*he clicks his fingers*) like that.
Craig Eh?
Bruce If you're playing a game it's fairly crucial everyone knows it's started, OK? You can't just suddenly hit someone in the face and say "Well, I've started boxing, where were y'?"
Craig I'm not playing sprout tag. They're not for sprout tag.
Bruce *Well, why've y' brought frozen sprouts into the depot?*
Craig (*after a pause*) They're for the eyes.
Bruce (*looking across the abyss*) What?
Craig The eyes. It's his eyes, isn't it? I couldn't think of anything else for the eyes. It has to be these.
Bruce Why?
Craig Because his were green.
Bruce *Whose?*

Craig His! (*He suddenly produces a flan base covered in tin foil with two sprouts embedded in the front. And sadly, that is exactly what it looks like*)

Bruce I — am slightly alarmed you're referring to a flan base covered in tin foil with two sprouts prodded into it as "him".

Craig I've only just / started ——

Bruce I have to admit that worries me.

Craig No / I ——

Bruce Food depots are like hospitals, Craig. You can't get emotionally involved with the occupants.

Craig I'm not.

Bruce You've got to distance yourself from the food, mate.

Craig I / wasn't ——

Bruce We can't have you weeping "Come back and see me sometime, fellas" at the back of every truck that goes off.

Craig I'm not getting attached to the food. I'm calling it "him" because he was male, wasn't he? He was a "he".

Bruce Who?

Craig (*waving the flan base*) Akhen-Put-Ra! "The boy king." (*He waves the flan base*) "Boy". OK?

There is a pause

And he had green eyes. They were the most important thing. (*He calms a little*) I'm not bothering with this detail for the other bits. I was just going to use a Mars bar for the mouth. That'll be all right, won't it? (*He looks up*) D'you think people'll be able to recognize him from the eyes?

Bruce looks at Akhen-Put-Ra. Then back at Craig

Bruce Put it this way. If he snatched my handbag, I'm sure I'd be able to pick him out in an identity parade.

Craig *It's not for an identity parade.* I mean for us. To recognize. It's not supposed to be real. He didn't look like this in real life.

Bruce Good.

Craig It's not a sculpture. It's not life-like, is it?

Bruce Well, y' never know. "King Akhen-Put-Ra" might be Egyptian for "King Disconnected Flan Head".

Craig It is connected. Well it will be.

Bruce To what?

Craig To his body.

Bruce (*quietly*) Oh no.

Craig Well, he's an icon. I had to make him a body.

And out of the reserves Craig rears up the rather extraordinary sight of a silver body, rather angular, made up of rectangular boxes and a central larger rectangular box, all wrapped in shiny tin foil. It looks like a headless robot that's just gone through a car wash

Bruce's eyes widen slightly

(*Matter-of-factly*) I mean once I've worked out how to get the head on, we'll be away.

There is a slight pause

Bruce (*quiet and measured, trying to be calm*) You are, I hope, aware the last person to say that sentence was Dr Frankenstein.
Craig What?
Bruce Exactly — where will you "be away", Craig?
Craig The game! What I thought is, as part of the clues, I could say that all the reserves in the depot, OK, were the mountain caves of Foum-el-Hassan.

Bruce starts to make a low moaning noise

So one of them had to have the treasure of Akhen-Put-Ra. Because they look like that don't they. If you look ... (*he leans over the railing*) the sheer face that you have to climb up to — wh-urps —— (*he nearly falls, hanging on to the side Dexion*)
Bruce Cr-urgh. (*He closes his eyes*)
Craig (*carrying on, unflurried*) — to get to, it's like loads of different caves ...
Bruce Craig, get away from the edge.
Craig (*sitting again*) So we can do the actual excavation!
Bruce Craig. (*He is like a father going to erupt*) Am I right in thinking King Akhen-Put-Ra is predominantly packet soup?
Craig Who?
Bruce Am I right in thinking that if you dropped King Akhen-Put-Ra into the Nile he would turn it into eight hundred miles of Batchelors Highland Lentil?
Craig Well these are / yeh, it's ——
Bruce (*shouting*) What are you playing at, Craig?

Craig never likes being shouted at

Craig It doesn't have to be so real / istic ——

Bruce Why, Craig / have you ——
Craig The eyes are enough for the clue.
Bruce I'm not talking about the accuracy of the model, Craig. I'm fairly sure King Akhen-Put-Ra didn't look like that, 'cause there was no flaming Akhen-Put-Ra! He's part of a dinner party board game that comes in a box! He is not born of noble lineage. He was invented by two blokes with red specs sitting in an office in London.
Craig I know that / I ——
Bruce Y've broken into a unit on the reserves!
Craig I / know ——
Bruce We can't do that, Craig, we can't explain that one away.
Craig I know he's not / real ——
Bruce We can't say it was bashed by a picking cage up here, can we?
Craig It's / not ——
Bruce A picking cage couldn't've split it open up here, could it?
Craig No / I know ——
Bruce So why've you done it?
Craig 'Cause they were high up, it says in the game.
Bruce The game's finished!
Craig What?
Bruce Robbo's solved it.

There is a slight pause

Craig (*shutting this out*) He can't've.
Bruce He got all the clues.
Craig There might be others.
Bruce (*grittily*) We've finished the cards.
Craig Ah, well, y' don't just stick to what's on the / cards ——
Bruce And if it's ended, people aren't going to carry on playing, are they?
Craig (*the lights go on in his mind; pointing*) Aha, right. And it's not, yet. 'Cause it ends when the solution card gets read out.
Bruce I'm going to do that now.
Craig When everyone's got all their accusations.
Bruce I am just about to get the solution card. I am just about to read out who-dun-it ——
Craig No, well, that's why we have to carry on. Or we won't get the who-dun-it.
Bruce (*quieter*) What d'you mean?
Craig Finding the who-dun-it card is part of the game.
Bruce (*quietly*) It's not.
Craig It is now.

There is a pause

(*Smiling triumphantly*) You see, King Akhen-Put-Ra isn't entirely packet
soup.

Bruce (*quietly and murderously*) Give me that game box.

Craig Bruce ...

Bruce *Take that tin foil off and give me the game box back.*

Craig Bruce ——

Bruce *It's my sister's game.*

Craig And it's carrying on.

Bruce *It isn't!*

Craig It *is.*

Bruce *Why?*

Craig (*suddenly shouting*) *Because I want it to!* Don't *shout* at me! Because
it's nice!

Bruce (*easing back instantly*) OK, I'm not / shouting ——

Craig *It's just nice! I like it.*

Bruce Craig ——

Craig *You don't stop if it's nice, and — and* ——

Bruce Craig ——

Craig And it's *Dr Costello*. Until it's finished.

There is a pause. Craig starts fiddling with the head again

Bruce (*sotto voce*) Oh-oh.

Craig If I lie it down the head'll stay on I suppose.

Bruce O — K. (*He shifts into police psychologist mode*) Crai ... Doct ... (*He
checks himself*) OK. Will the person in there please confirm for me that he
knows he is not really Dr Damon Costello?

Craig (*looking up; like a patient parent*) Bruce, I'm not stupid.

Bruce Good. That's a good start. Not being stupid is a great place to start.
Could he tell me next, OK, that he is under no impression that he at any
point did actually fight off a large Egyptian and make love to a beautiful
red-headed woman on a boat jetty in the River Nile?

Craig (*looking at him*) Look, I'm not a kid. OK. I don't think it's real, I don't
care about — about — the woman or fighting the Egyptian or who found
Akhen-Put-Ra or who killed the bloke in the railway carriage. And I don't
think I'm Dr Costello. (*He pauses slightly*) I don't even think I like Dr
Costello. I bet he'd be a real nobhead if you ever met him.

Bruce Well, why d'y' want to carry on, Craig?

Craig Because everyone listens to him. (*He looks at Bruce*) Everyone says
his things. (*He looks at the head*) They say his things. It's nice that. Like
you with "Tragically", how everyone's started saying that. And "Good
eh". "Wha-hey". I said that thing about the jug, and other people said it. It
is nice that, isn't it?

Bruce looks down into the abyss again

Bruce We could carry on. Craig. We could for a bit. But we'd have to stop sometime.

There is a pause

Craig I know that.

Bruce They're not happy people, you know.

Craig Who?

Bruce (*nodding*) Who want to be something different. 'Cause it doesn't stop anywhere. There's always something different that comes up on the horizon when y've got to Buxton and y' just keep going, mate. Tromping these massive distances, and that's all you do. (*He pauses slightly*) You want to be happy with — with / what ——

Craig (*nodding to himself*) What you are.

Bruce Well, yeh.

Craig Have you ever thought it might be easier to do that if y'r a Bruce Kenny not a Craig Cleminson?

Bruce "Where" you are doesn't matter, Craig.

Craig It does. If you're up there with the Bruce Kennys and Damon Costellos ——

Bruce It's got nothing to do with being "up" anywhere.

Craig It does, I know now.

Bruce No.

Craig I know what it feels like ——

Bruce Craig, I want you to believe me if I say something, will you?

Craig It is great, isn't it?

Bruce Being happy, Craig is very very simple, OK. 'Cause it's a distance, OK. Like that (*he measures one with his fingers*) distance. Discus throw distance between two points. (*He marks it out*) Where you are. And where you want to be. The most important thing y' ve got to do in y'r life is keep that distance as small as you can.

Craig (*turning to Bruce, dead serious*) You don't believe that.

Bruce Eh?

Craig You wouldn't be going for promotion if you believed that.

Bruce Craig ——

Craig I brought the letter for y', remember? You shouldn't do that.

Bruce Craig ——

Craig You do that to kids. Saying they have to do something while the grown-ups do something different ——

Bruce Craig, hold the flan base out.

Craig Y're not having it.

Bruce I'm not taking it. I want to give / you ——
Craig You do that to / kids ——
Bruce Craig!
Craig "Do as I say not as I do", isn't it?
Bruce Oh, you little berk.
Craig "Do as I say, not as I ... what're y' doing?
Bruce R-r-right!

With a bound, Bruce jumps from the catwalk to the fifth reserve,

Craig shoots back in horror. Bruce stands in the fifth reserve like Batman having just crashed into a baddies' lair

Craig You can't get into the mountain caves like that.
Bruce (*quietly gritted*) Craig. Guess what I've got in my pocket.

Bruce hands back the letter. Craig looks at it

As Li Ho Ping said. Shut up and read.

Craig does

You'll notice the phrasing is " ...we have secured you a place on the management induction course ... ", not " ... your application has been successful ...". 'Cause there wasn't one. They decided for me. Apparently I have a natural sense of responsibility. It says in the paragraph about being a natural team-leader.
Craig (*looking up*) This is bad news?
Bruce Well it is right now, 'cause I can't just say "no", can I, y' see. They'll be ferreting round, bobbing up and down round here trying to convince me and we can't have that. That'll wreck the games. I've been thinking it all out, mate. Believe me, I don't know how I get out of that letter yet.
Craig But y' really want to say no?
Bruce (*looking at Craig*) Craig. Tomorrow is the final of the flan discus. What the hell do I want promotion for?
Craig The flan discus? (*He's tempted*) Is it?
Bruce (*nodding*) It would be. But we can't start another game till we've finished this one.
Craig (*looking at the head of Akhen-Put-Ra*) Right. Well I'd better not carry it on then, had I?
Bruce Better not.
Craig Better get rid of it, then.
Bruce Better had.

Craig hands the letter back. Bruce folds it up during the following

Craig (*with a vague smile*) 'Cause I could start now, couldn't I?
Bruce Getting rid of it? You could, mate.
Craig Yeh. Well, both things. I could do both at once.
Bruce Mm?
Craig Training as well. 'Cause it's about the right size.
Bruce What is?
Craig (*beaming*) Fifty-foot drop — that'll train y' to stay in the circle.
Bruce What are / you ——?
Craig Ta-ra Akhen-Put-Ra. Hallo Chin-knee-toe.
Bruce Come away ——
Craig Make a bow, see it ——
Bruce *Craig - gg!!*

Craig swings his arm back in order to throw the head of Akhen-Put-ra like a discus off the reserve

Soaring music. Black-out

Scene 8

The Depot. A day later — Friday night

A spotlight comes up on Bruce standing on the food

Bruce Nothing happens once, does it?

The Lights come up to reveal the other lads, gathering round the depot like Benny and the others in "Top Cat". They sit exactly as they were at the very start of the play. It's like the whole thing never happened

In here. And then disappears. Once something's happened in this place, that's it. It's flaming trapped. For ever. (*He walks into the middle of the floor*) It'll just keep coming round again. Like unclaimed baggage.

There is a pause. The music stops

So. (*He pauses*) Did anyone see her actually get hit?

A shaking of heads, as in ACT I SCENE 1

All Nrr.
Bruce Who found her?

Ewan (*half-looking up; guiltily*) I — er — but I didn't see her get hit. She was already on the ground. (*He pauses*) When I got to her.

Bruce Robbo, did ...(*louder*) Robbo, did you see it?

Robbo I heard this shout and then I saw these jars rolling down the end of E. She fell back into the sandwich spread. It was a half-empty pallet. Her hand went through one of the slats.

Bruce (*wincing*) Ff-ff. (*He pauses slightly*) Poor old Debbie.

There is a pause

Craig It's my fault. I forgot I'd made the eyes out of sprouts. They must've shot out.

Dids It's the only way one could've hit her that hard. Coming down from really high up. I mean to get it that fast down here y'd have to be throwing 'em, and no-one was doing that, were they?

Ewan No. (*Quietly*) No, it must've shot out.

Bruce It was like having a terrible movie replayed in front of you. It was like "Glen Two. The Sprout Strikes Back".

There is a slight pause

Ewan (*shrugging;quietly*) And then there were five.

Craig Are we going to say it was another industrial injury?

Bruce No. I couldn't, Craig. Not this time. I had to make a decision. And I made it.

Craig What've y' done?

Bruce It was me that started the game. If you start the game, you take responsibility. That's the rules.

Ewan You told them ——

Bruce The truth. Miss Petley was injured attempting to stop a game being played in the depot on Thursday night which I, Bruce Kenny, had instigated. End of report. (*He shrugs*)

Craig You took the rap?

Dids "Took the rap?"

Craig What?

Dids People stopped "taking the rap" when they stopped saying "it's a fair cop, guv."

Craig But he went in and said it was his / fault ——

Bruce Anyway. (*He pauses slightly*) The next award, ladies and gentlemen, of the Bruce Kenny Trophy, will be organized and presented by Craig.

Dids Eh?

Bruce Well, are you doing the flan discus or not?

Craig Oh, yeh. *Yeh.*

Dids Discus?

Craig Oh yeh. Well we need things. We need the bases.
Bruce (*nodding to the others*) This is his one. Do what he says. Go on.

Everyone except Ewan gets up and ambles for the exit

Bruce (*louder*) Flan bases, Robbo.
Robbo Where's the flan bases?
Dids F-thirty-four-A.
Craig Right, but we need the medium size ones, not the party size.
Dids L-thirty-five-B.

Everyone exits except Ewan and Bruce

Ewan Great. And so it's — I mean, flan discus, it's back like before, yeh?
Bruce (*looking at Ewan*) What?
Ewan Well, just — you know. The games. We're kind of back on the games-with-everything like before. (*He smiles*) Again.
Bruce Course it is.
Ewan Course it is. Yeh.

Ewan exits

Bruce sits. He looks at the Bruce Kenny trophy. He polishes it a bit with his sleeve

Debbie (*off*) You know that's tragic.

Bruce looks up

(*Off*) People who sit staring at old trophies is sad enough. Staring at ones they've bought themselves is tragic.

Debbie enters with her coat on. Her wrist is in plaster and there is a mark on her head

Bruce (*looks at Debbie, then at the trophy*) It's got a picture of a squash player on. That's even worse.
Debbie You do know it's your fault, this is.
Bruce What?
Debbie That I've started saying the word "tragic" all the time. (*She holds the plaster up*) When she was putting this on the nurse asked what hit me, and I said "Tragically, I have no idea."
Bruce Right.

Debbie It's a good job I'm not staying down here. It's only a matter of time before I'd be shouting "Good eh" and "Wha-hey".

Bruce (*nodding*) I should've given y'r stuff to the ambulance bloke.

Debbie 'S OK. I had to come in anyway.

Bruce Oh yeh?

Debbie Yeh, the — er — (*she nods upwards*) I got a summons.

Bruce Not the little office in the sky?

Debbie (*smiling*) Mm.

Bruce And what did the little men in the little office in the sky have to say?

Debbie Oh. (*She shakes her head*) Nothing. No, it was just …

Bruce Come on, dear, spit it out.

Debbie That a place has suddenly come free. On the induction course.

There is a pause

Bruce You got it?

Debbie Looks like it.

There is a pause

Bruce So. You're off.

Debbie I'm off.

Bruce Buxton. Glossop. Twenty years you'll be in Matlock.

Debbie (*smiling*) You don't mind me telling you this?

Bruce Eh?

Debbie Sorry. Looks a bit bad. I did come to say t'ra, not to say like "I've got promotion and you ..." (*she nods*) y' know.

Bruce Oh, nah. Don't worry.

Debbie Y' re not bothered.

Bruce No. Well. (*He smiles*) Yeh actually. Would've been good to have you down here a bit, but —— (*he shrugs*)

There is a pause

Well. (*He stands and holds his hand out to Debbie*) See y' then.

Debbie It's broken in eight places, Bruce.

Bruce Right.

Bruce shakes Debbie's unbroken hand

My gran always said if you shake hands with your wrong hand ——

Debbie Don't tell me. If it's bad news, I don't want to know.

Bruce OK.

Debbie Leave me guessing.

There is a pause

Bruce Have fun.
Debbie See y', Bruce.

She goes

Immediately Craig twitters back on with several flan bases

Craig (*holding out a base to Bruce*) Right. OK Bruce, there you go. That's yours.

Bruce takes the flan base from Craig, still looking off in the direction taken by Debbie

Ewan enters with his flan base; Dids and Robbo enter and Craig doles bases out to them in the corner

Craig (*calling*) Did you get the markers, Robbo?
Robbo Yeh, well I got the tuna back out the recoup area.
Craig OK, OK. And when you measure it, you always mark the spot where it lands.
Robbo From shove tuna.
Craig Not where it skids to. That doesn't count.
Ewan So listen — they're — er — not going to do anything are they?
Bruce (*turning*) Mm?
Ewan Management. About the sprout thing. It wasn't your fault really. I mean, you didn't do it, like.
Bruce Yeh, well.
Ewan Are they going to fine y'?
Bruce (*pulling on a smile*) It wasn't mentioned.
Craig Right, Bruce? Ewan? Are you ready to learn the turn, yeh?
Dids Who's first?
Craig No-one yet. You haven't learned how to do it yet. The first thing is you have to spend a moment getting used to having it in y'r hand.

They all stand getting used to the flan bases

Ewan So they're not taking any action at all?
Bruce Oh yeh. Yeh. (*He shrugs*) I'm afraid I am no longer deemed responsible enough for a place on the management induction course, Ewan. That's the price I have paid.

Craig After me.

Bruce I am afraid whilst others may eventually rise to soar above the Sierra Madre, I'm lumped with staying down here on the animal shift.

Craig Good, eh? Right, and after me!

Bruce (*turning and beaming at Ewan*) Life is so tragic.

Craig Are you ready?

Ewan (*smiling*) Isn't it. Tragic.

Bruce Tragic.

Craig Are you ready? OK, and ready with the poem, right?

Bruce (*on full octane again*) *I'm ready Craig! We're all ready, Craig! Wha-hey!*

Craig *Good eh? Chin knee toe* ——

The others join in

All Make a bow — See it go—o ——

And as their arms go back, high octane, ebullient music snaps in

Black-out

FURNITURE AND PROPERTY LIST

On stage throughout: Pallets holding boxes of food including: pesto sauce, Fudge, Smarties, tuna steaks

ACT I
SCENE 1

No additional props required

SCENE 2

Off stage: Picking cages (**Ewan** and **Dids**)
                 Small frozen fish (**Ewan**)
                 Two small frozen fish (**Dids**)

Personal: **Robbo**: scarf
                 Craig: scarf

SCENE 3

Set: Picking cages and labels for **Bruce** and **Ewan**
                 "Muscle and Fitness" magazine for **Dids**
                 Three small frozen fish for **Craig**

Off stage: Picking cage (**Robbo**)
                 Boxed flan base (**Craig**)

SCENE 4

Set: Open box of Smarties
                 Smarties and tube lid for **Ewan** and **Bruce**
                 Flan base

SCENE 5

On stage: Damaged crate of tinned tuna steaks
                 Picking cage for **Bruce**

Set: Tinned tuna steak (**Robbo**)

Personal: **Craig**: letter

SCENE 6

Off stage: Chocolate bar (**Dids**)
Plastic bag containing small trophy (**Bruce**)
Plastic cup (**Ewan**)
Plastic bag containing "tweeter" trumpet from a stereo speaker (**Robbo**)
Nectarine (**Craig**)
Electric tip truck with bell (**Debbie**)

SCENE 7

No additional props required

SCENE 8

Off stage: Picking cage and labels (**Debbie, Craig** and **Ewan**)

SCENE 9

No additional props required

SCENE 10

Off stage: Picking cage and trophy (**Debbie**)

Personal: **Robbo**: remote control unit

SCENE 11

Off stage: Remote control unit (**Debbie**)

Personal: **Bruce**: cigarettes, matches
Debbie: packet of gum

SCENE 12

Set: Tweeter-trumpet speakers (practical)
Six A4 envelopes containing cards for **Bruce**

Personal: **Bruce**: remote control

ACT II
SCENE 1

Off stage: Picking cages and labels (**Dids, Craig, Ewan, Robbo, Bruce**)
                Electric tip truck(**Debbie**)

SCENE 2

Set: Torch for **Bruce**

Off stage: Electric tip truck, J-cloth (**Robbo**)

SCENE 3

No additional props required

SCENE 4

No additional props required

SCENE 5

Off stage: Frozen sprout (**Ewan**)

Personal: **Debbie**: packet of gum
                Bruce: packet of cigarettes, matches

SCENE 6

Set: Frozen sprout

Off stage: Flan base (**Dids**)
                Finger of Fudge (**Debbie**)
                Sprouts (**Bruce, Ewan, Debbie**)

SCENE 7

Set: Stacks of boxes including boxes of packet soup
                Flan base face (see description p. 75)
                Silver body (see description p. 76/77)

Personal: **Craig**: letter

Scene 8

Set: Trophy for **Bruce**

Off stage: Several flan cases (**Craig**)
               Flan base (**Ewan**)

LIGHTING PLOT

Practical fittings required: nil
Composite set: a warehouse on three levels and the roof

ACT I
To open: General interior lighting on Depot

Cue 1	"Eye of the Tiger" plays *Black-out*	(Page 2)
Cue 2	When ready *Snap up lights on Depot*	(Page 3)
Cue 3	**Bruce**: "... in tomorrow's papers." *Black-out*	(Page 5)
Cue 4	When ready *Bring up lights on Depot*	(Page 6)
Cue 5	**Dids**: "Bloody tragic." *Black-out*	(Page 12)
Cue 6	When ready *Bring up lights on Depot*	(Page 13)
Cue 7	**Bruce**: "... hide-and-seek with him." *Black-out*	(Page 15)
Cue 8	**Robbo** (*off*): "Arghhh — hh ..." *Bring up lights on Depot*	(Page 15)
Cue 9	Music plays *Black-out*	(Page 19)
Cue 10	When ready *Bring up lights on Depot*	(Page 20)
Cue 11	**Bruce**: "That was Debbie Petley." *Black-out*	(Page 30)
Cue 12	**Bruce**: "That girl was Debbie Petley." *Bring up lights on Catwalk*	(Page 31)

Cue 13	**Bruce** and **Ewan** look down *Crossfade to Depot*	(Page 32)
Cue 14	**Dids** (*singing*): "Walking through the Branston Pickle ... " *Crossfade to Catwalk*	(Page 33)
Cue 15	**Ewan** and **Bruce** leave *Crossfade to Depot*	(Page 34)
Cue 16	**Debbie** looks at **Craig** and **Robbo** *Black-out*	(Page 36)
Cue 17	When ready *Bring up lights behind skylight and fire door with overhead cover*	(Page 36)
Cue 18	**Bruce** beams *Black-out*	(Page 42)
Cue 19	**Voice 2**: " ... Marrakesh to Tangiers." *Bring up lights on Depot*	(Page 43)
Cue 20	Train effects and music blare out *Black-out*	(Page 45)

ACT II
To open: General interior lights on Depot

Cue 21	**Robbo**: "So why were you in Marrakesh?" *Black-out*	(Page 57)
Cue 22	**Bruce** switches on the main lights *Snap on lights in Depot*	(Page 58)
Cue 23	**Bruce**: "Shazam!" He clicks his fingers *Black-out*	(Page 63)
Cue 24	When ready *Bring up lights on Catwalk*	(Page 63)
Cue 25	**Debbie**: "What are you like?" *Crossfade to Depot*	(Page 64)

Cue 26	**Craig** exits with his Fudge bars *Black-out*	(Page 66)
Cue 27	When ready *Bring up lights behind skylight and fire door* *with overhead cover*	(Page 66)
Cue 28	Big swirl of music *Black-out*	(Page 71)
Cue 29	When ready *Bring up lights on depot*	(Page 71)
Cue 30	Big, eerie music *Black-out*	(Page 74)
Cue 31	When ready *Bring up lights on Fifth Reserve*	(Page 75)
Cue 32	**Craig** swings his arm back *Black-out*	(Page 82)
Cue 33	When ready *Bring up spotlight on* **Bruce** *in Depot*	(Page 82)
Cue 34	**Bruce**: "Nothing happens once, does it?" *Bring up lights on Depot*	(Page 82)
Cue 35	The men's arms go back for the throw *Black-out*	(Page 87)

EFFECTS PLOT

ACT I

Cue 1	**Bruce**: *"Wha-hey!"* *"Eye of the Tiger" plays*	(Page 2)
Cue 2	**Bruce** stops singing and speaks *Snap off "Eye of the Tiger"*	(Page 3)
Cue 3	**Bruce**: "...flames licking off the back?" *Bell rings*	(Page 16)
Cue 4	**Bruce** drums his fingers on the letter *Music plays*	(Page 19)
Cue 5	When ready *Fade music*	(Page 20)
Cue 6	**Debbie** exits; **Bruce** looks after her *Music plays*	(Page 30)
Cue 7	When ready *Fade music*	(Page 31)
Cue 8	**Debbie** presses a button on the remote *Brass band plays in the distance*	(Page 37)
Cue 9	**Debbie** presses a button on the remote *Cut brass band music*	(Page 38)
Cue 10	Opening of SCENE 12 *Recorded voice and music over practical speakers as pp. 43-44*	(Page 43)
Cue 11	**Bruce** presses a button on the remote control *Train effects and music over practical speakers*	(Page 45)

ACT II

Cue 12	Black-out *Train and whistle effects*	(Page 57)
Cue 13	When ready *Fade train and whistle effects*	(Page 58)

| *Cue* 14 | Black-out | (Page 63) |
| | *Sinister music* | |

| *Cue* 15 | When ready | (Page 63) |
| | *Fade music* | |

| *Cue* 16 | Craig: "It's the rules." | (Page 66) |
| | *Music* | |

| *Cue* 17 | When ready | (Page 66) |
| | *Fade music* | |

| *Cue* 18 | **Ewan** throws an object on the floor | (Page 71) |
| | *Ominous music* | |

| *Cue* 19 | **Ewan**: "There's frozen sprouts in the warehouse." | (Page 71) |
| | *Music: "Dum dugger dum", then big swirl of music* | |

| *Cue* 20 | **Bruce**, **Ewan** and **Debbie** look at the sprout | (Page 71) |
| | *Fade music* | |

| *Cue* 21 | **Ewan** exits | (Page 74) |
| | *Big, eerie music* | |

| *Cue* 22 | **Craig** starts up | (Page 75) |
| | *Snap off music* | |

| *Cue* 23 | **Craig** swings his arm back | (Page 82) |
| | *Soaring music* | |

| *Cue* 24 | **Bruce**: "Like unclaimed baggage." | (Page 82) |
| | *Fade music* | |

| *Cue* 25 | The men's throwing arms go back | (Page 87) |
| | *High-octane, ebullient music* | |

A: act 2 scene 1

B: Tempest

C: Blythe